High Shelf

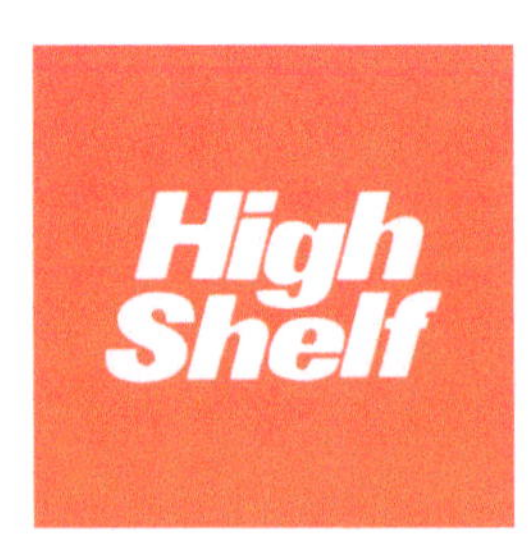

High Shelf XXXVI. November 2021.
Portland, Oregon.
Copyright 2021, High Shelf Press

ISBN: 978-1-952869-46-4

Cover Image by Andrés Porras
Editing, Design and Layout by C. M. Tollefson

With special thanks to:
David Seung & Eric Hoskins

High Shelf XXXVI

November 2021

“... Flesh, callous
In selfish pursuit
I fly away blind, drawn to new rot... ”
Josephine Pino

"... As Bonaventure noted, you find god by going deep
within, and you get within from without,
exploring the natural impression of things and how..."
S. T. Brant

Table Of Contents

My Anti-Vax Poem

Juan Cortez

I never understood how the flu came back every year.

Was it because doctors gave shots in the arm?

Do they not know a shot to the heart kills a man?

The Father of Gynecology tasked to save black slaves

value. Child breeding or working the fields, birth complications

made it either or. Four years and twelve slaves later, he solved it.

Anarcha, Betsy, Lucy. Only three named. Where are their thank yous?

Apologies? Words worth nothing. Monster of gynecology.

Fathers don't experiment on their daughters.

Now black women are six times more likely to die on the table.

Have they lost their value?

Black men given syphilis, cut apart, disembodied,

brains dissected on live bodies, dead stolen from graves.

But I'm supposed to trust white doctors today?

Black people, vax your kids. They need it.

Curious however, white families spearheading the anti-vax campaign.

Where are your horror stories? The monsters in your own family.

This body was a body

Jamie Avery

before it was a crime scene. This body
was landscape and hillside, was fresh rain

and dew. This body was journey, sweat-
damp and longing, and honestly? It's hard

being the sad girl when I'm wet with all this
want. And sure, sometimes I wish you'd killed

me, but it's too late for that now. I'm stuck in
this body, earthside and hungry, so I check

myself out in car window tint. I wolf-whistle
at myself in the 7-11 parking lot. I slap my ass

in the mirror, and I call it healing. I forgive my
softness for the ways it couldn't save me, and

sun-nap like it's the weekend. I carry my body
to the water as an offering. I wait for it to rain.

Who Am I

Labdhi Shah

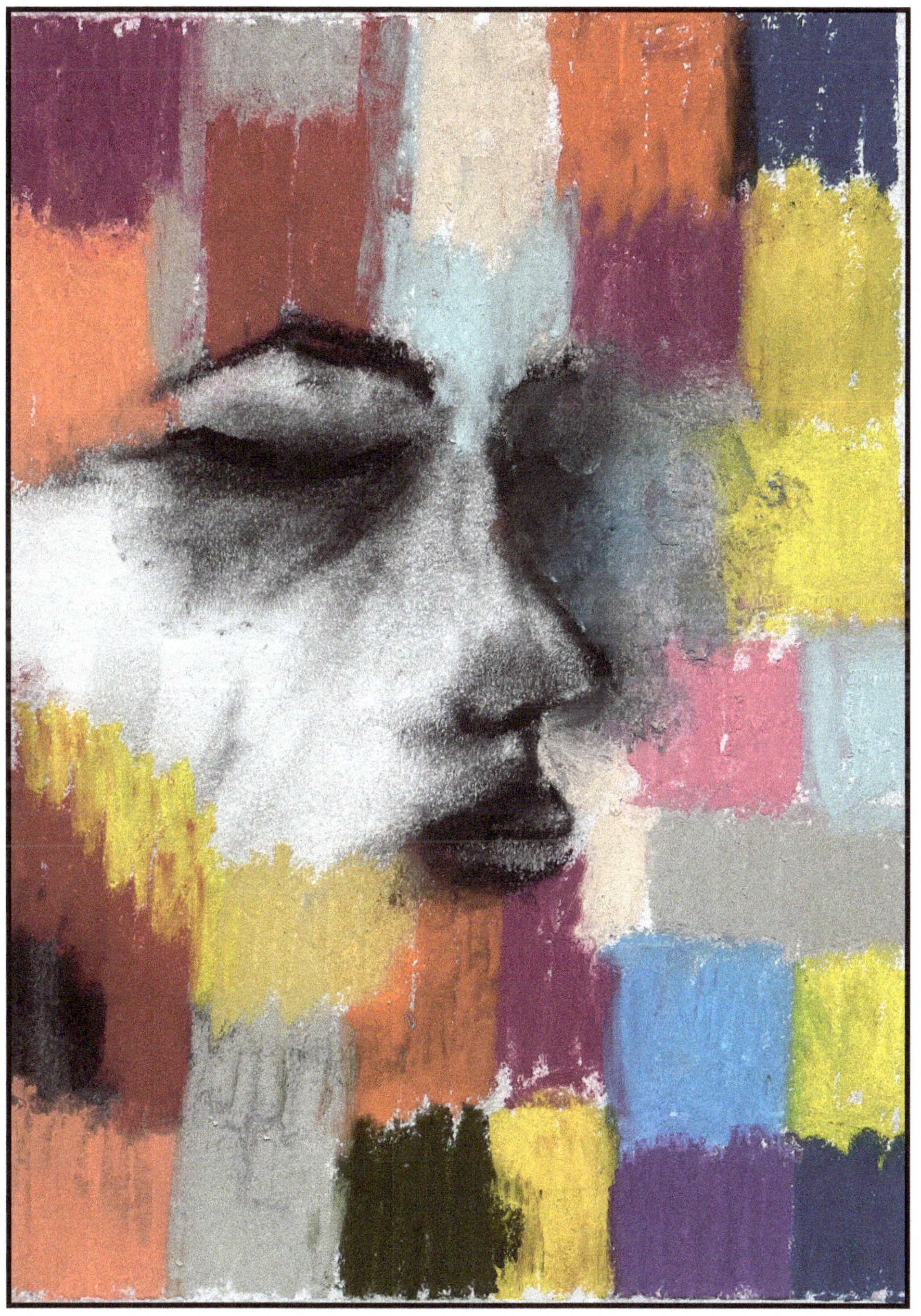

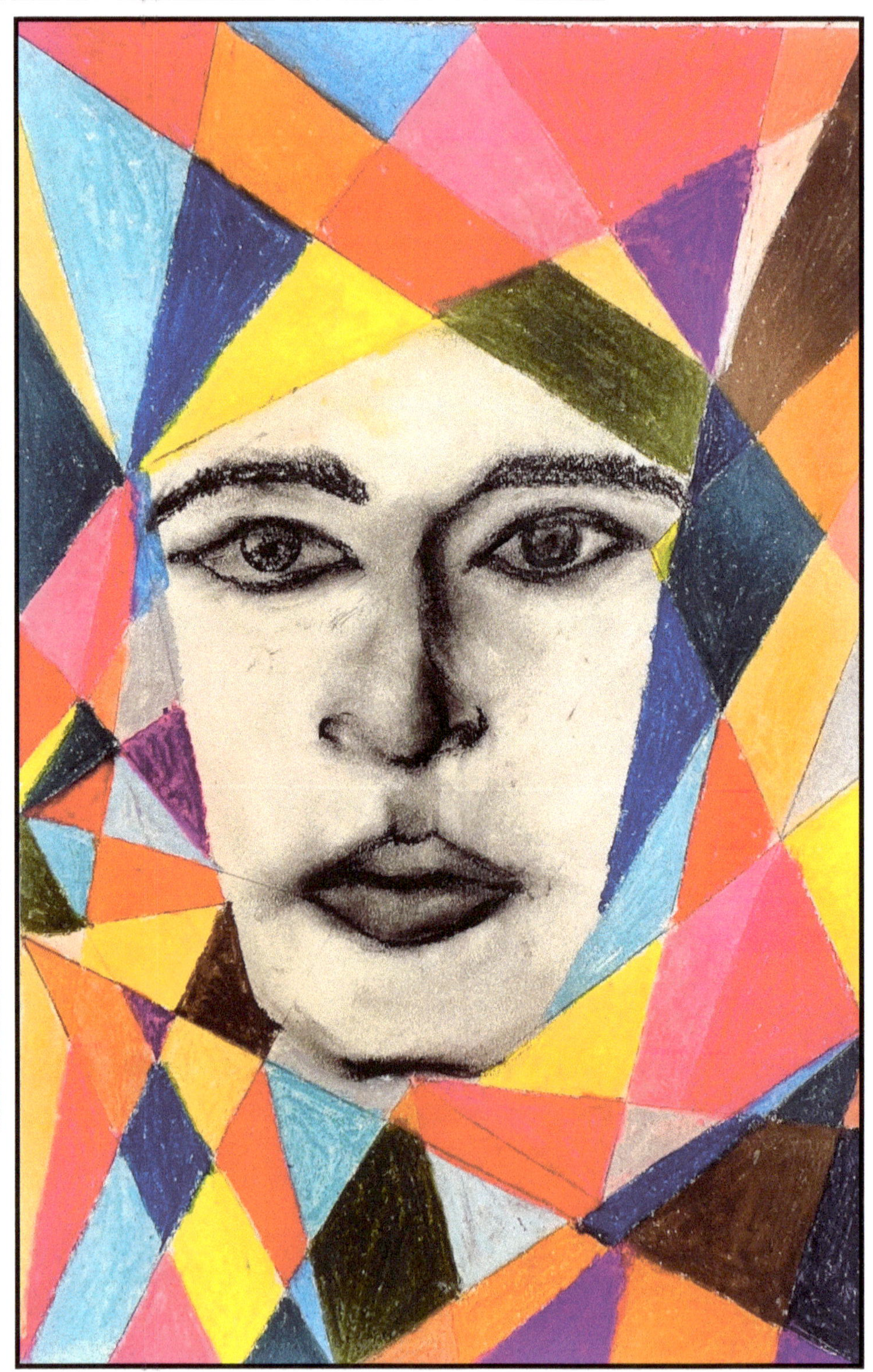

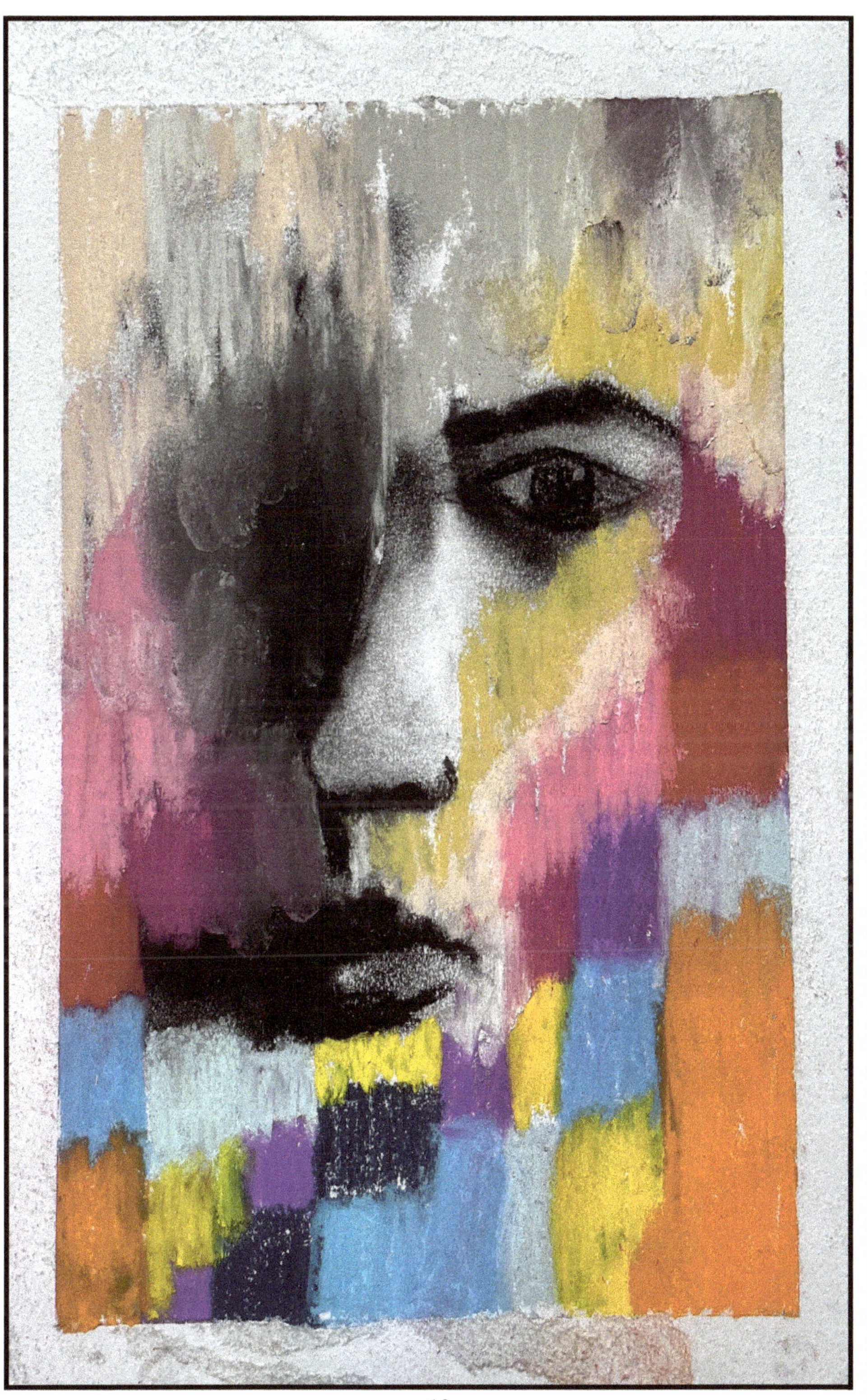

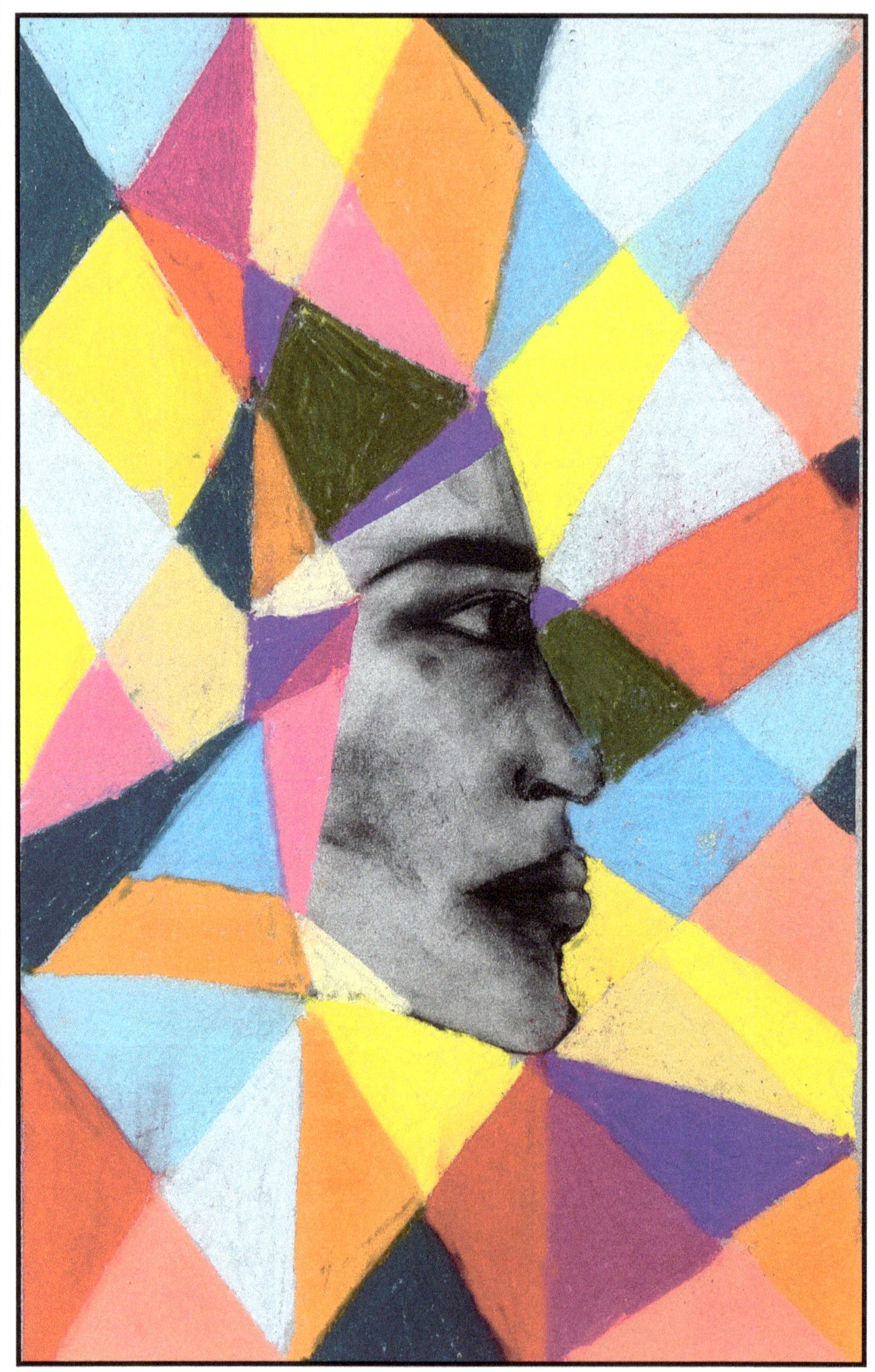

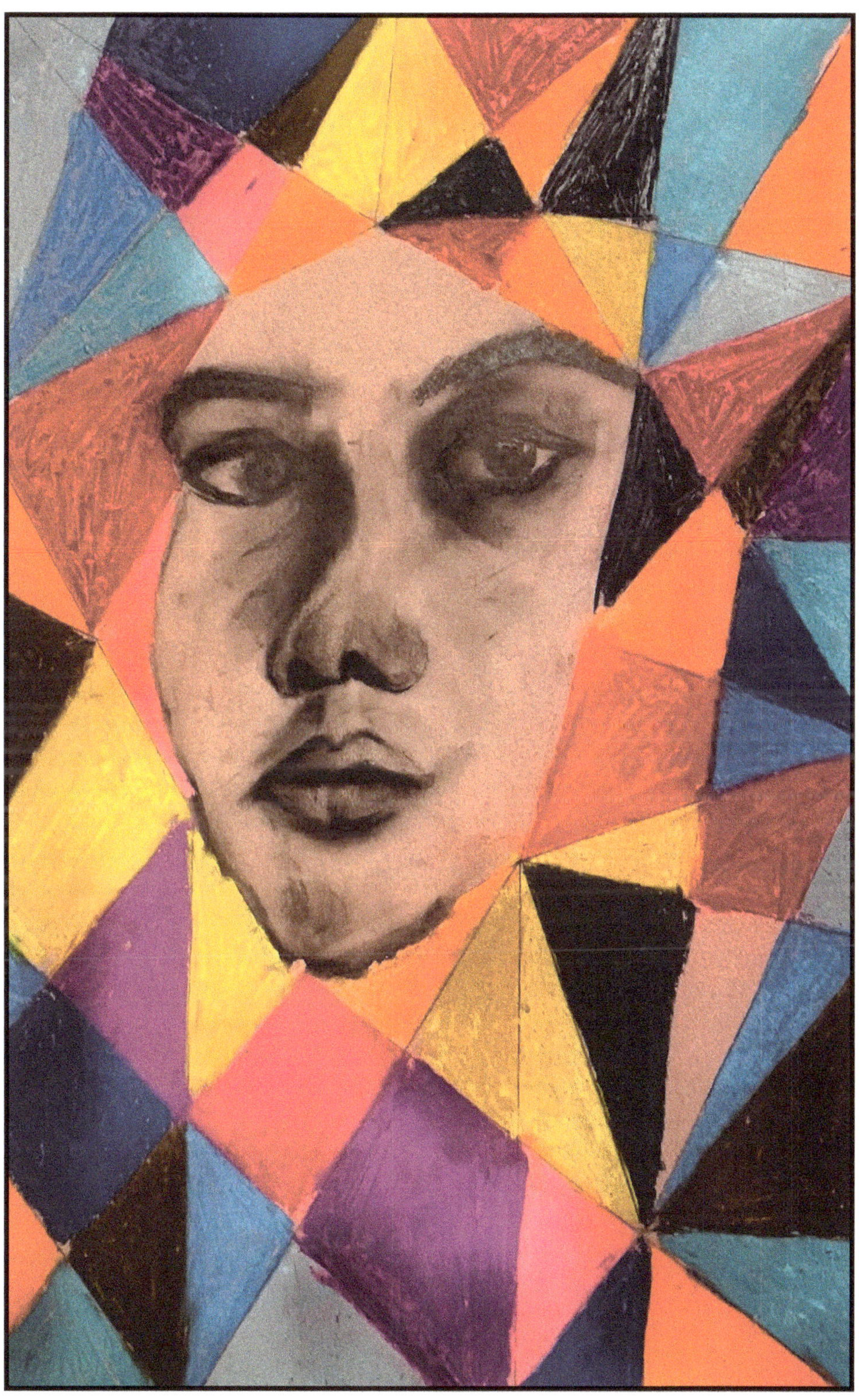

Botfly in Metamorphosis

Josephine Pino

"A great civilization is not conquered from without until it has destroyed itself from within."
~ Ariel and Will Durant

I rip my way
Toward light as I grow
In bestial gluttony

My hardening shell
Gunmetal grey over
Entrails digesting sound

Bites of decay
Bulging eyes
Peer ahead

Red-rimmed, despised

Sticky wings unfurl
Away from leaking

Flesh, callous
In selfish pursuit
I fly away blind, drawn to new rot

What I leave behind –
A gaping hole
Hemorrhaging edges. Pain

Penelope

Samantha Cramer

Sea-cliff pacing as fog
banks wait, my own dark sailed
armada.

I polish arrowheads
for a nameless war that
never comes;
bronze tipped death, and
silence.

my empire of thread and salt

This, and these, and all–
my pillow stuffed with pomegranate skin
and laurel.

I paint my eyelids gold,
marriage symbol
to a husband they have
never seen

even this, my sanctuary, a battlefield

Wind in lionmane hair, lips
bitten and raw, palms
open, and
empty

The sand cries out for blood.

The Space Between

Sophie Robson

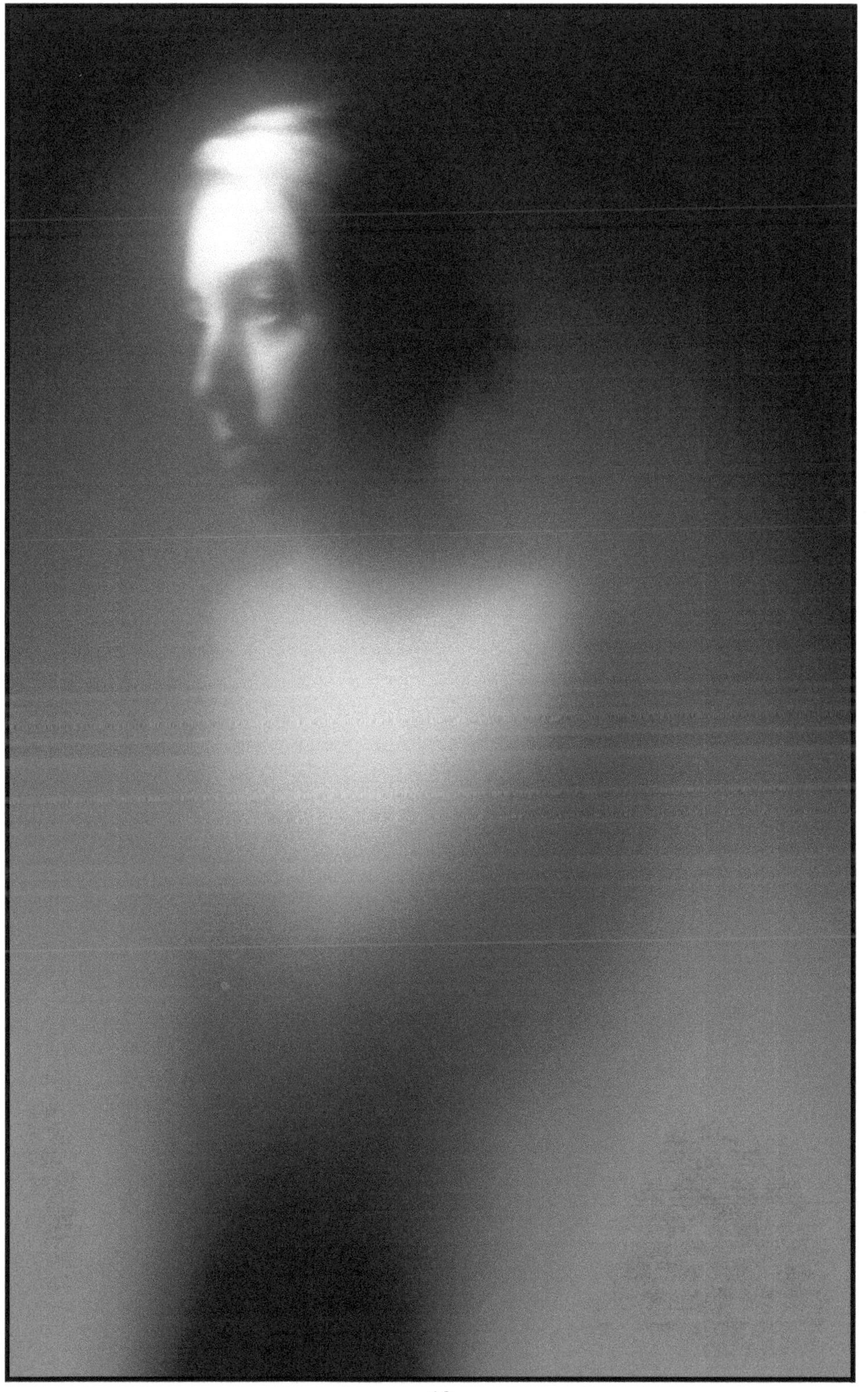

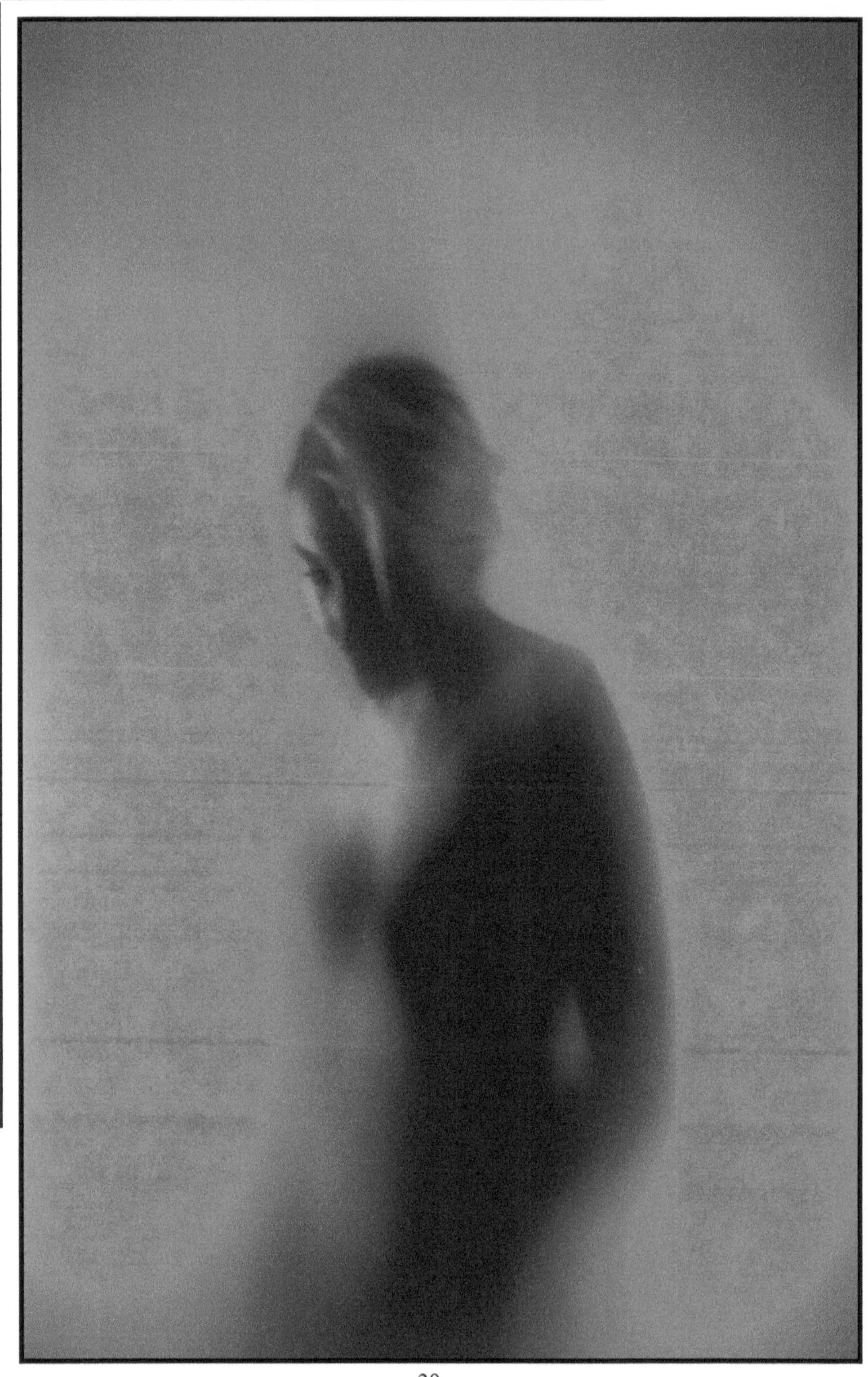

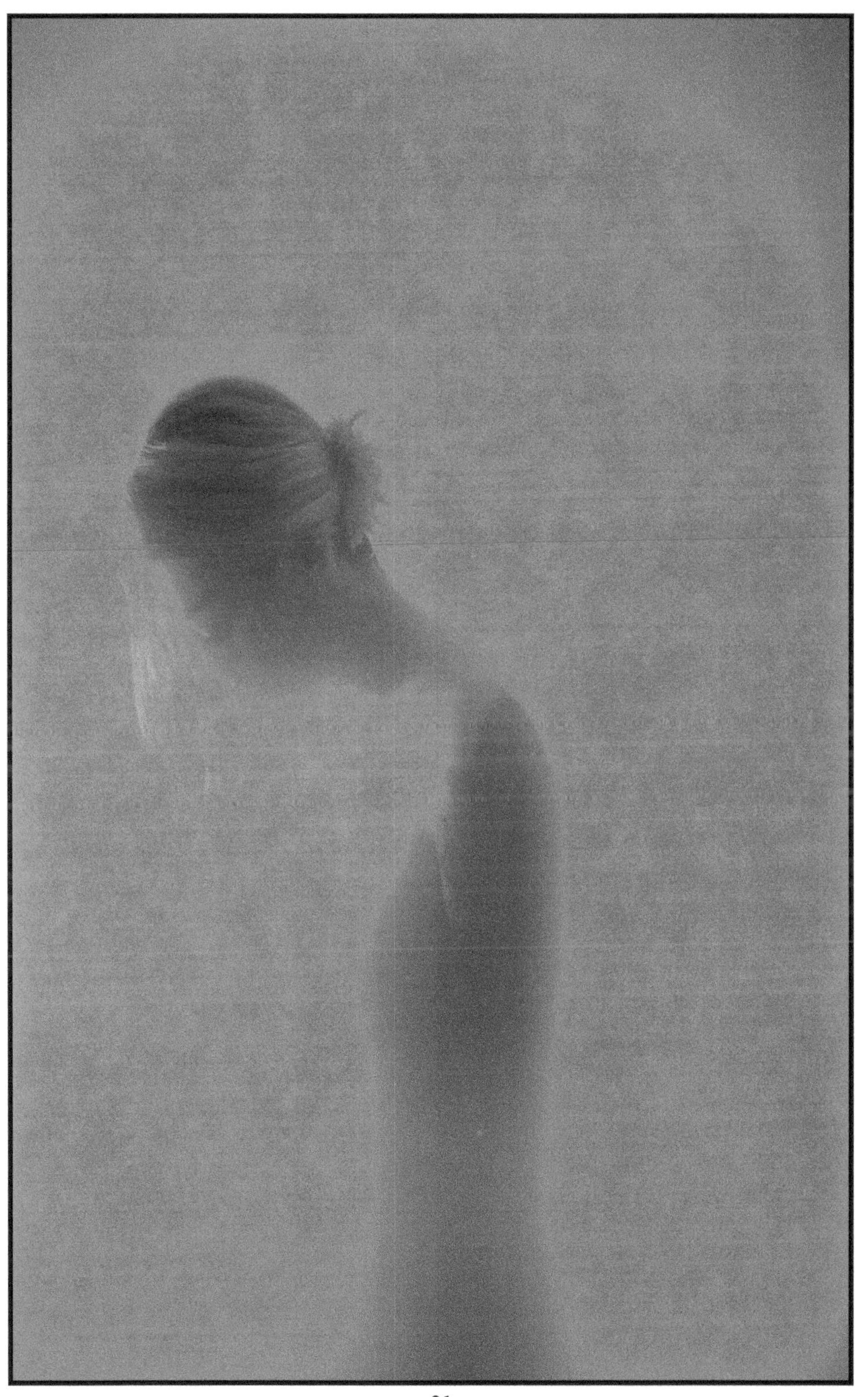

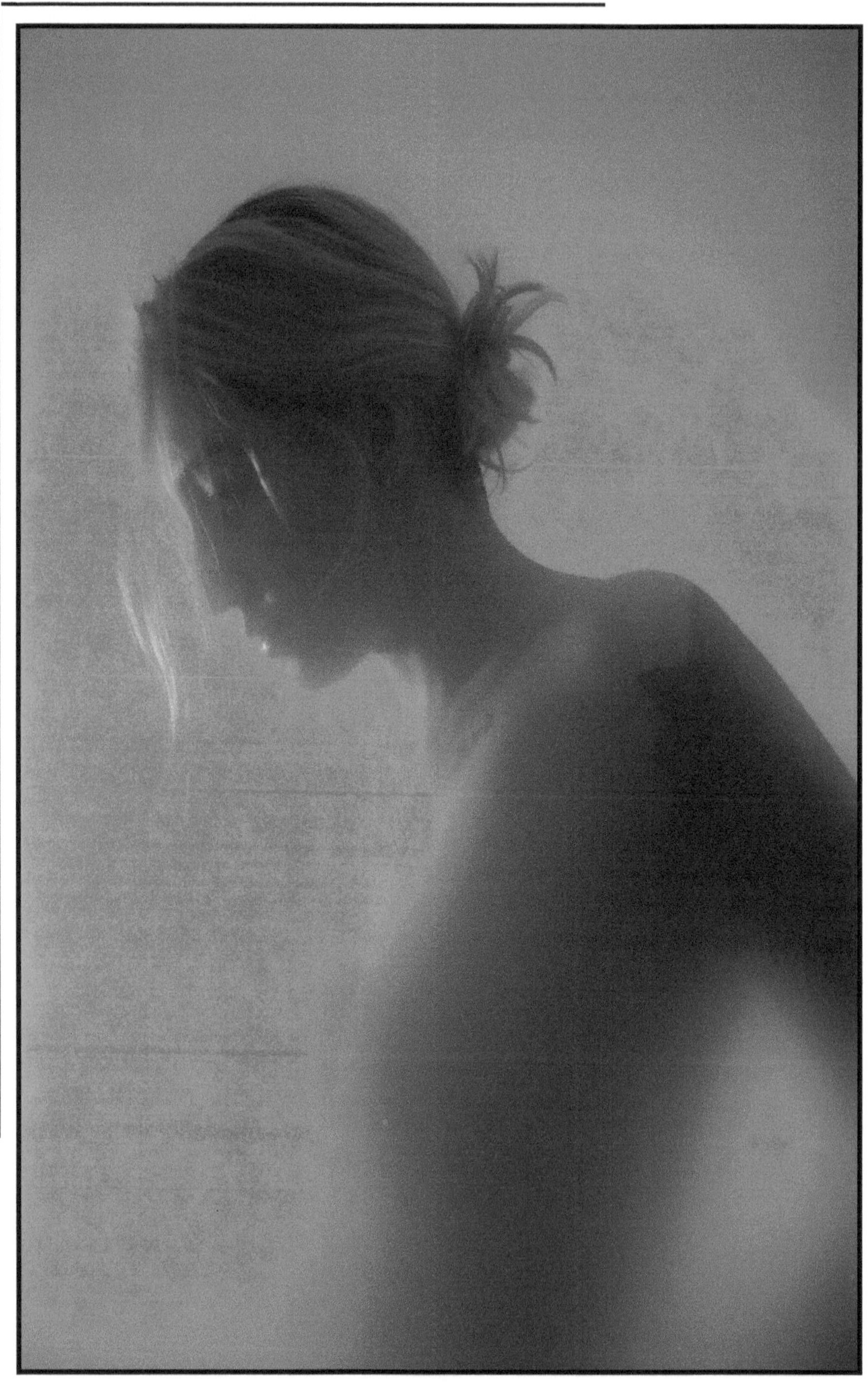

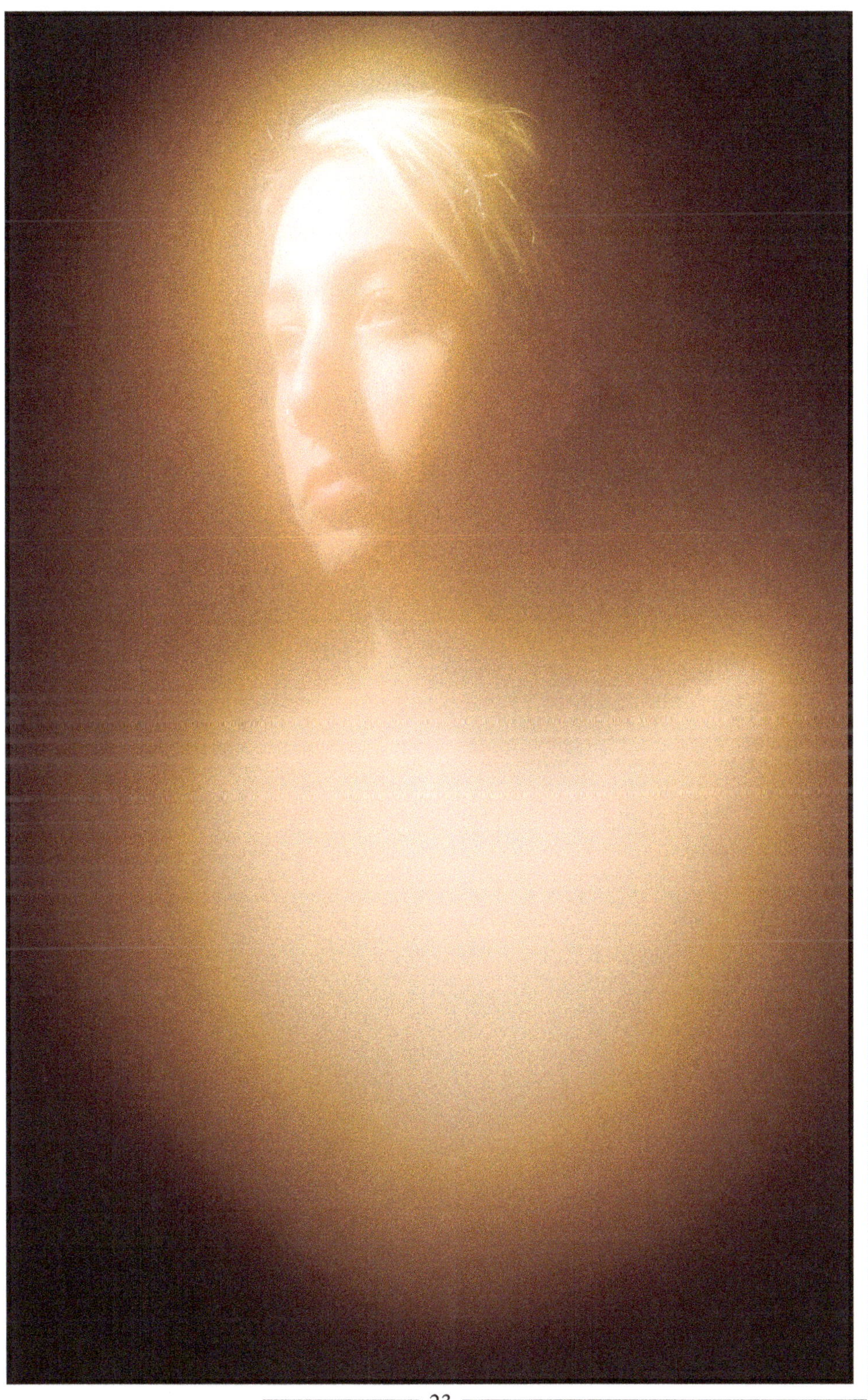

Scar Tissue

Sara Rempe

gut rust uterus rust cunt rust
a crust   this blood glues
rectum to uterus   appendix to ovary to scar
tissue   I can't survive the past
unless this man cuts me   pulls out
the ovary the dead rat I beg
my body   let go go slack
this stasis has been no rest

let him dig out the curse
let the irate tissues hiss   burned and snipped
he's in me and I watch
him tear through this webbed hell   watch him
project it on the wall
let it glow on our faces a cosmos   art
the snared silk crusting like salt

what are these pictures he has for me?
this language this curtsy this new arc of time?

a month is nothing blood
nothing pain nothing
body I've forgotten
my mind his fingers my cunt
my ass my language no longer
describes me here I am

staked
with slicked dildos   fit with cameras

spread pushed pinched pulled pressed
cut burned clipped sucked torn stitched his

language   left like a careless tool his *success*
stuck in my guts like darts
the sharp ends hit the most tender parts

Daylight Savings

Stella Saalman

It's sunset, and the sky has painted itself
as though it still thinks this will be the last one,
the last goodbye,
because they have all got it wrong and the sky is not a man
but a baby
with no object permanence and it cannot understand
that after a few hours of quiet darkness, the sun will come again.

You took so many photographs of it,
like our newborn, lost so many years ago;
and now all that's left of you
are thousands of shiny five-by-sevens,
each one different and yet the subject went unchanged,
an Impressionist tapestry that says nothing of who you were
but shows us all what you cared for.

I haven't decided what to do with them.
I'd like to put them in freezer bags, then plastic tubs,
store them away down the basement safe from oily fingerprints,
down where the sun doesn't shine
and I don't have to look at what's left of you.

But this is not what you wanted,

Taking shot after shot, every time the sun went down,
on the porch, in the yard, in the street
no matter where the night found us.

She liked sunsets, you used to remind me;
Clapping her hands and exclaiming over them,
because each one was new,
and she hadn't yet inherited my indifference—
and you liked that it was the two of you, proving me wrong,

That in truth each one was different, not just
in its moment of arrival, but in its form,
in its birth
in its life
in its death,
slipping away beneath the earth
until its rebirth the next morn.

It will be stained again tomorrow, but the sky cannot comprehend this.

The World Is Upside Down
Andrés Porras

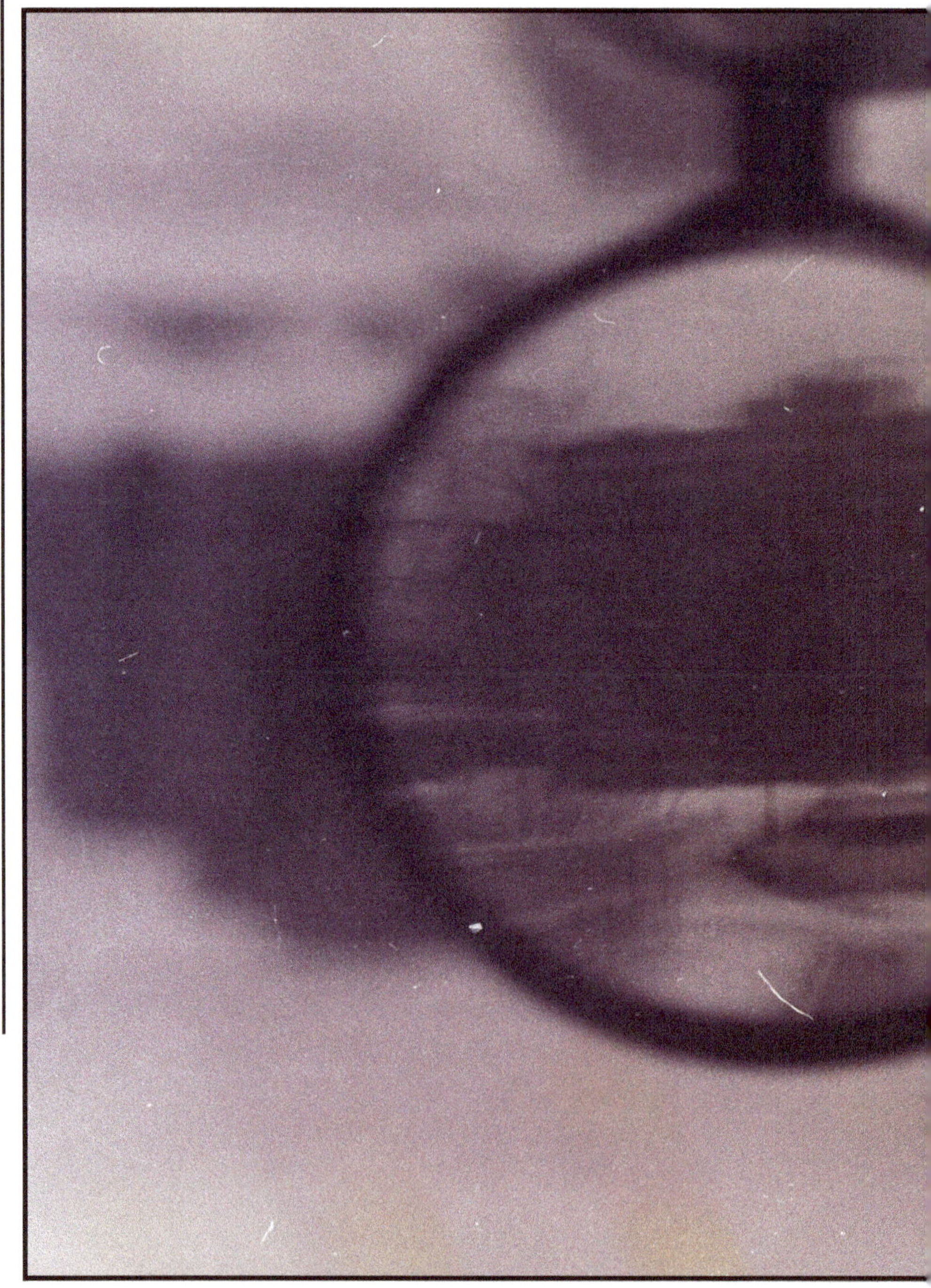

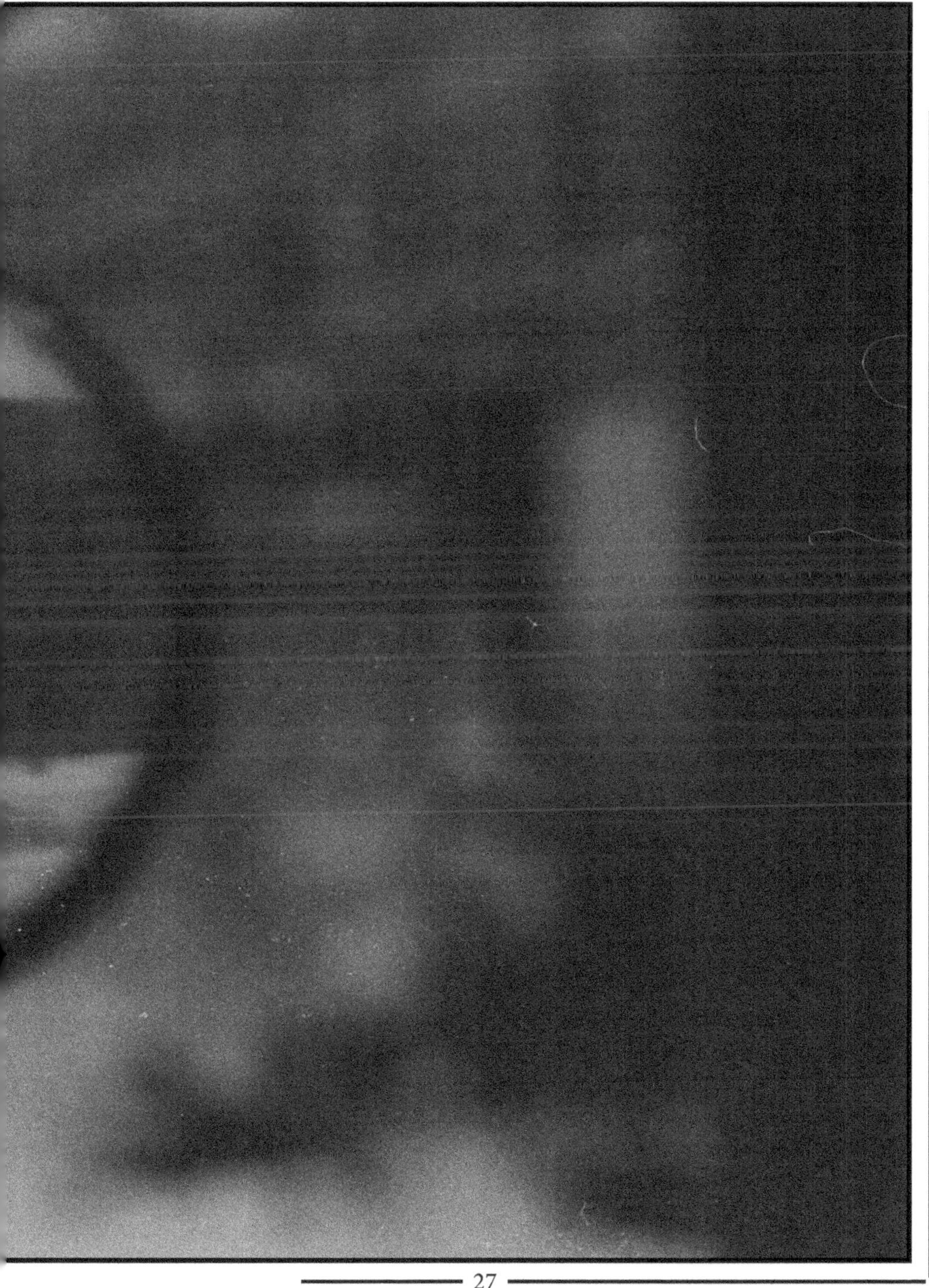

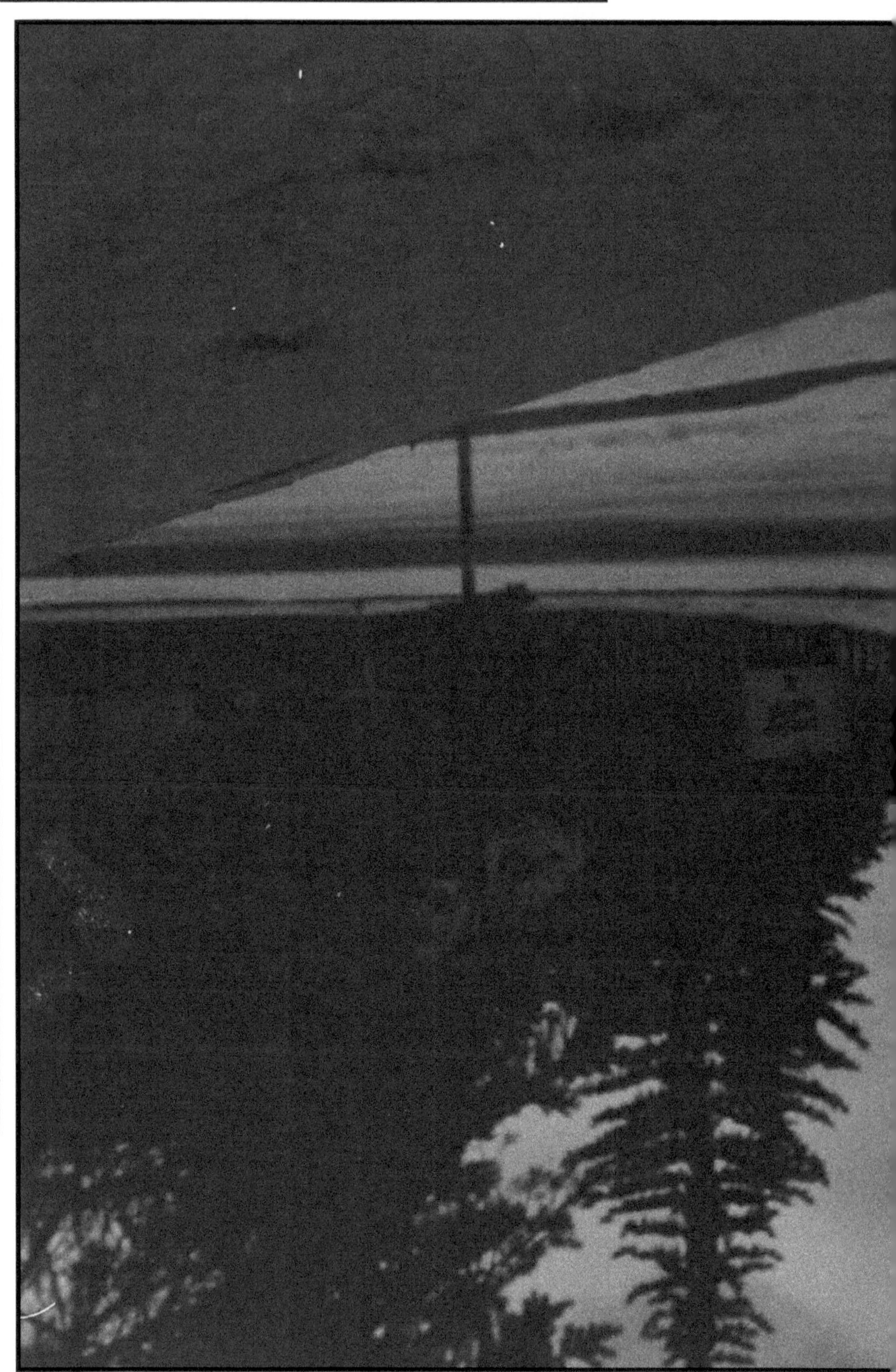

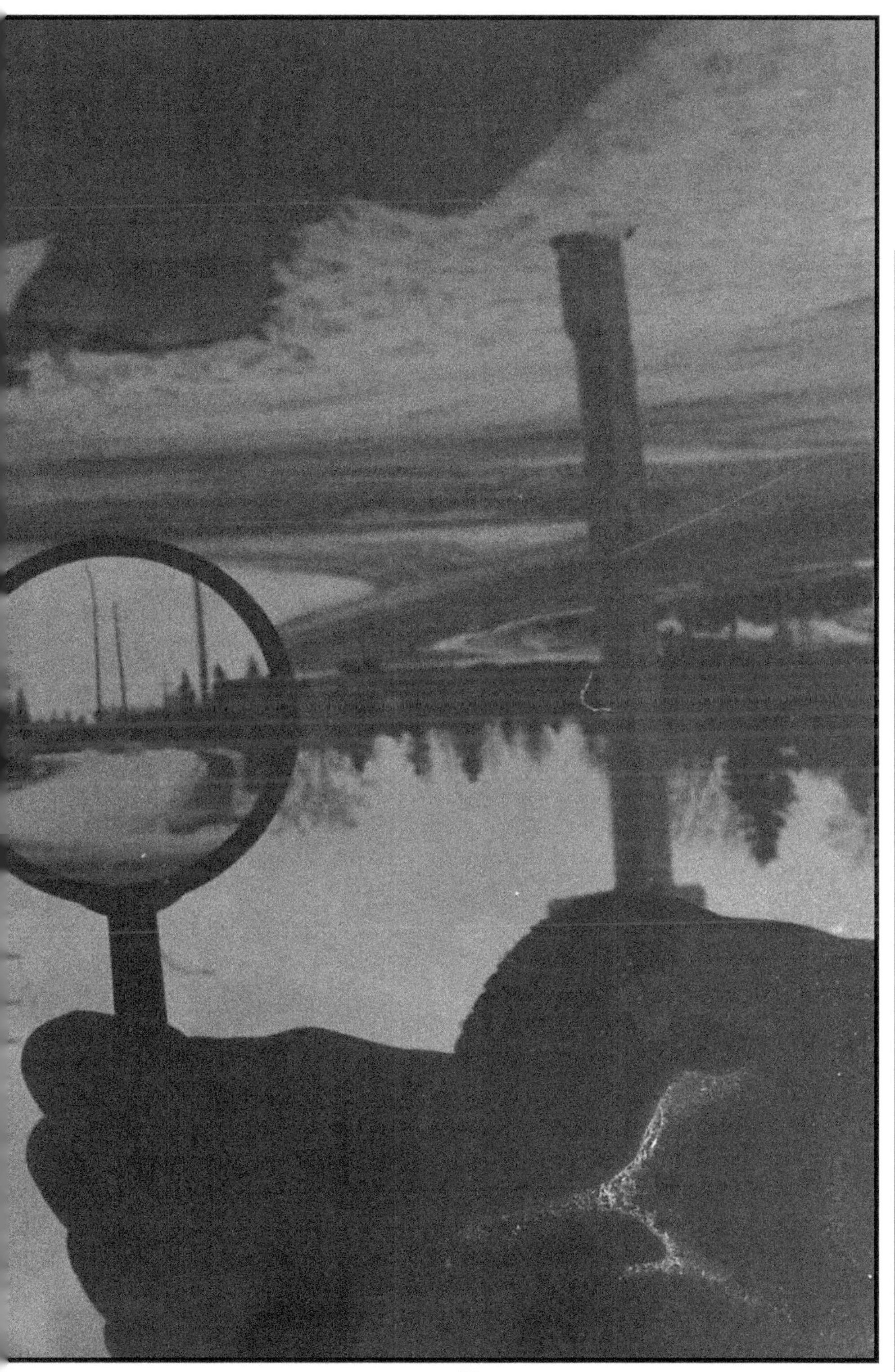

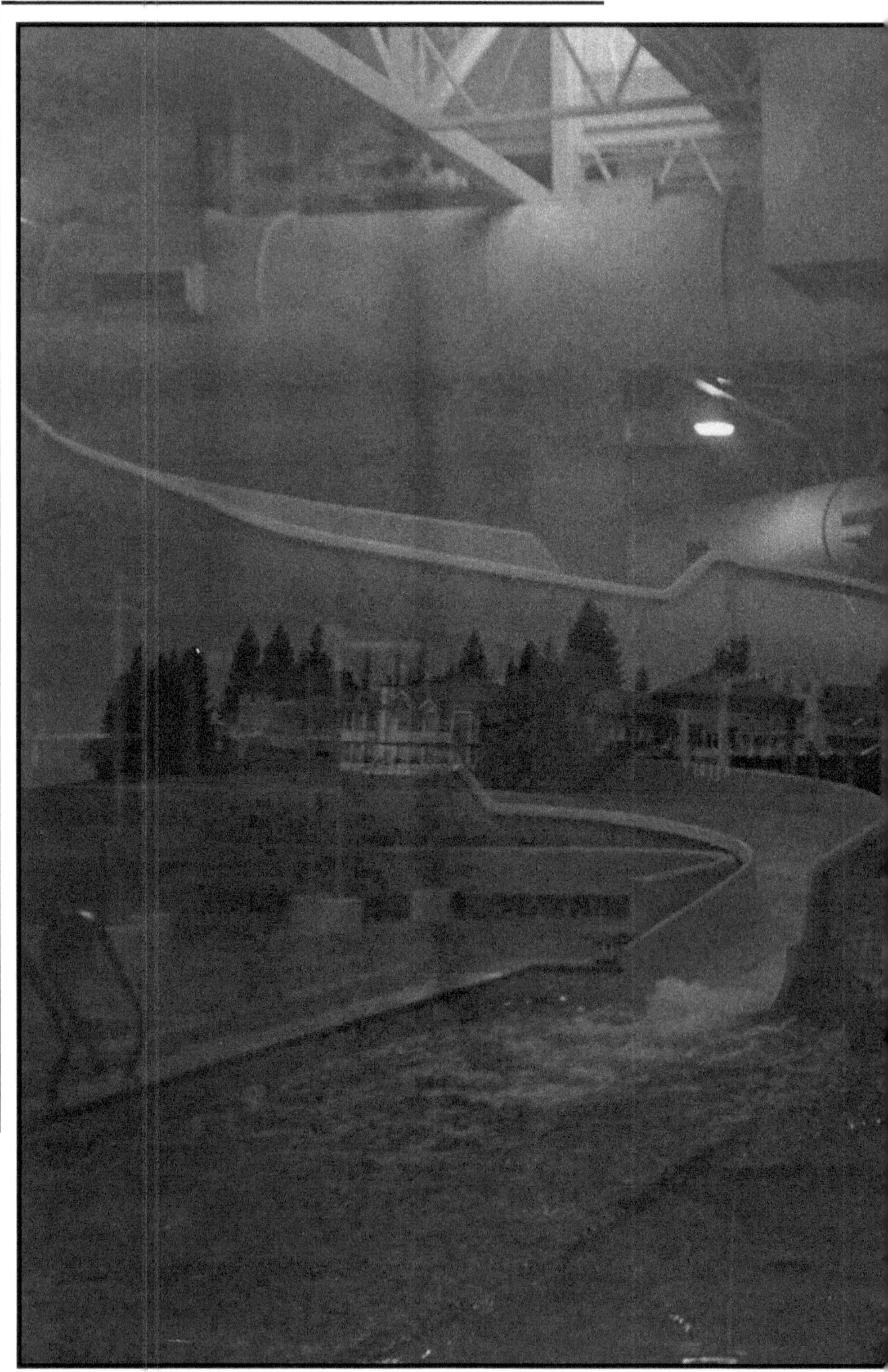

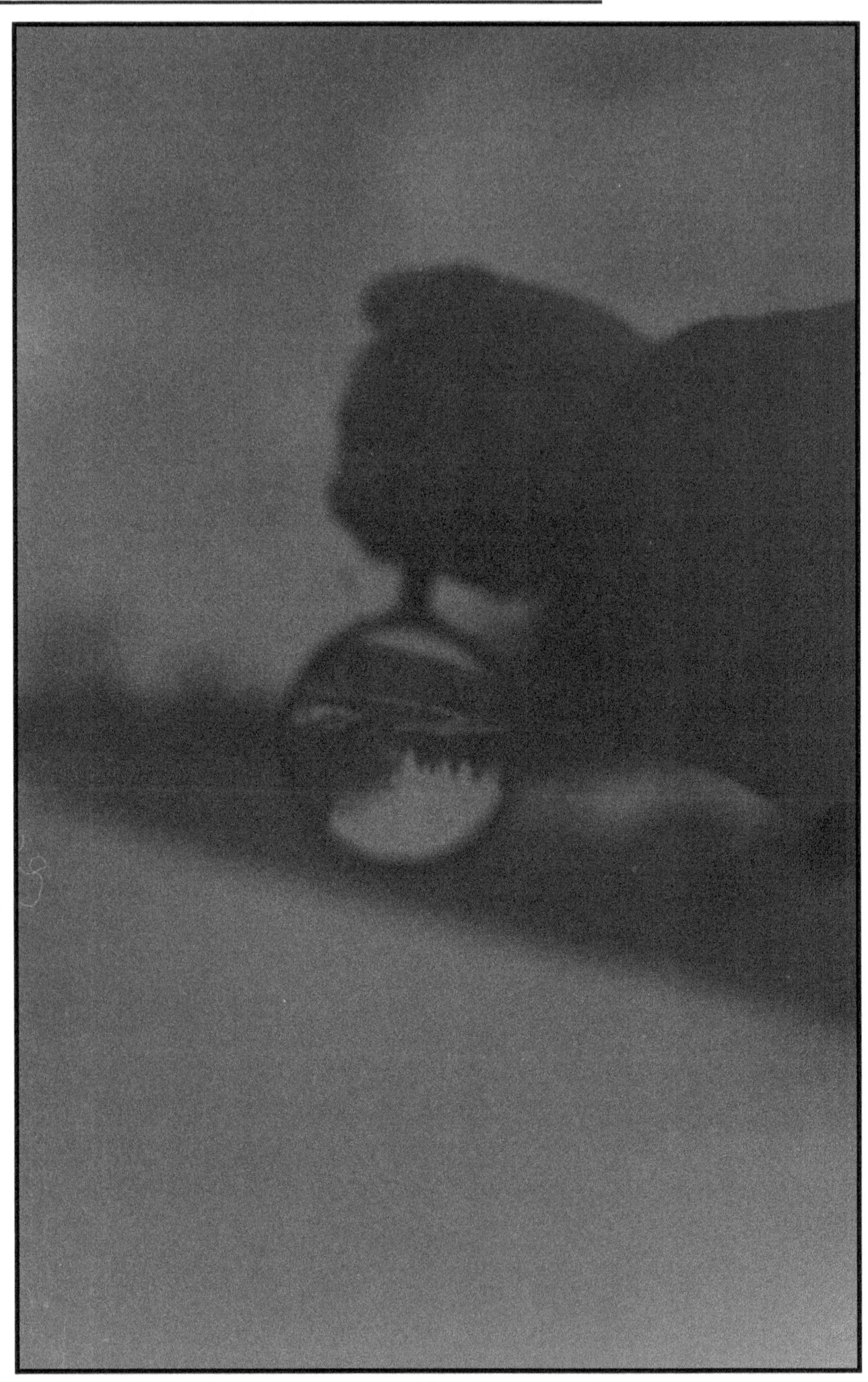

Boneflower

Sally Wilde

I plan the night garden, down to the last detail
A distraction from a leg cramp, or
The med tech bending, sterile paper rustling,
Cold metal or needles against skin, or the
Techno beat bashing as you lie so still
In the long white tube. You'll get out of here,
You remind yourself. Laboring over the imaginary garden
Is a way to not be here, now. My fear: I know
We won't have time to make the garden; we will never
Be granted that stretch of space to grow
Omixochitl, whose night scent young women
Are advised not to breathe. No such cautions
For old ones. Our gardens are choked
With weeds and frost-struck stems.
The table is a cold slab. I take my mind back
To details. Tuberose is a perennial in this climate
And will take a year. The roots are rhizomes.
I wonder: Can the bay overwinter?
Where will I get the seeds for the black poppies?
You would know, you would know. I dream myself away
To the place where I touch the boneflower
Blooming flesh-pale against the darkness,
In a few hours, coming. This could be
The only night garden we will know.
Only as big as this bed, in this room,
On the night ahead of us. This must be enough.

Seeking Isolation

Anthony Kelly

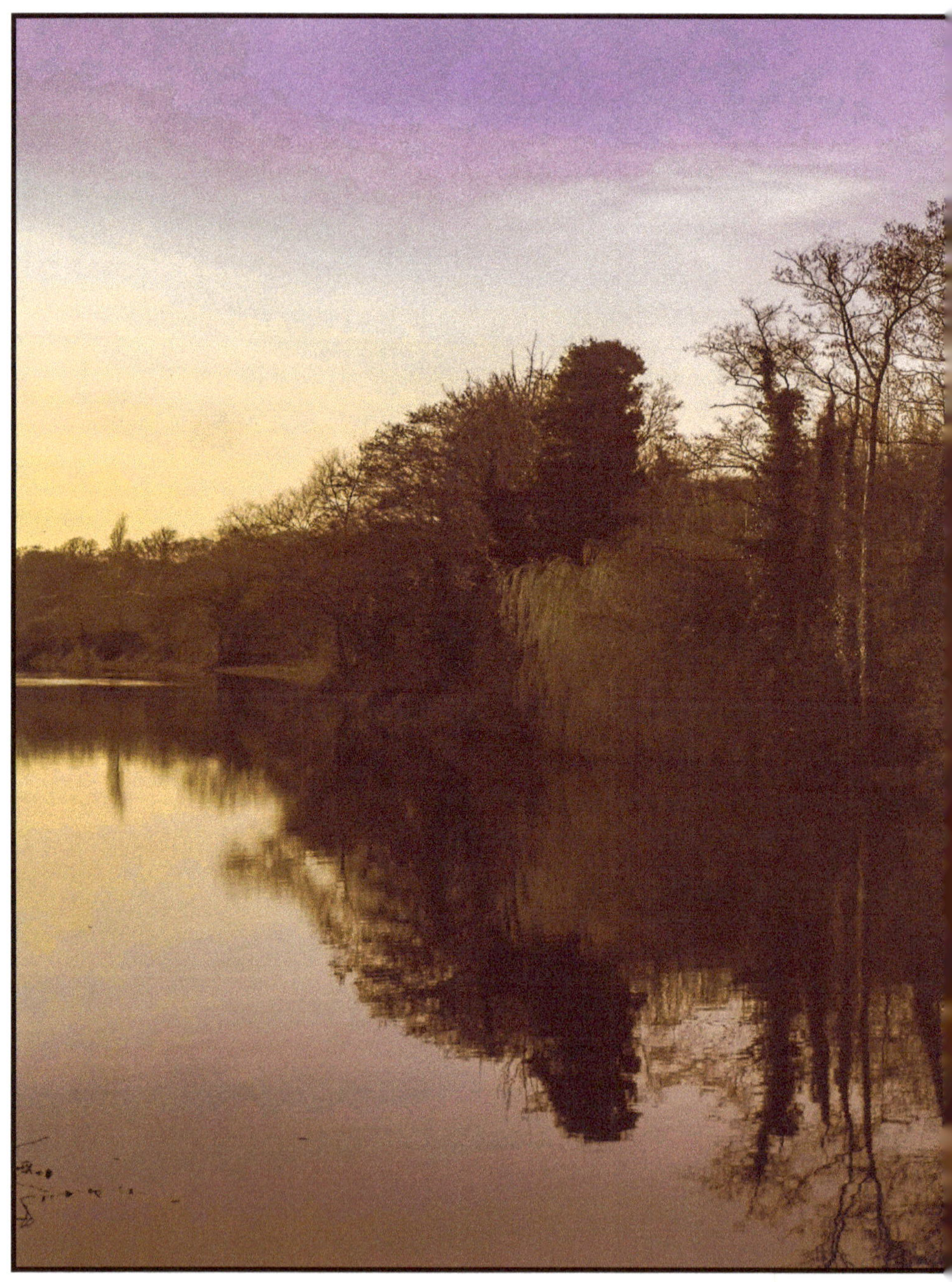

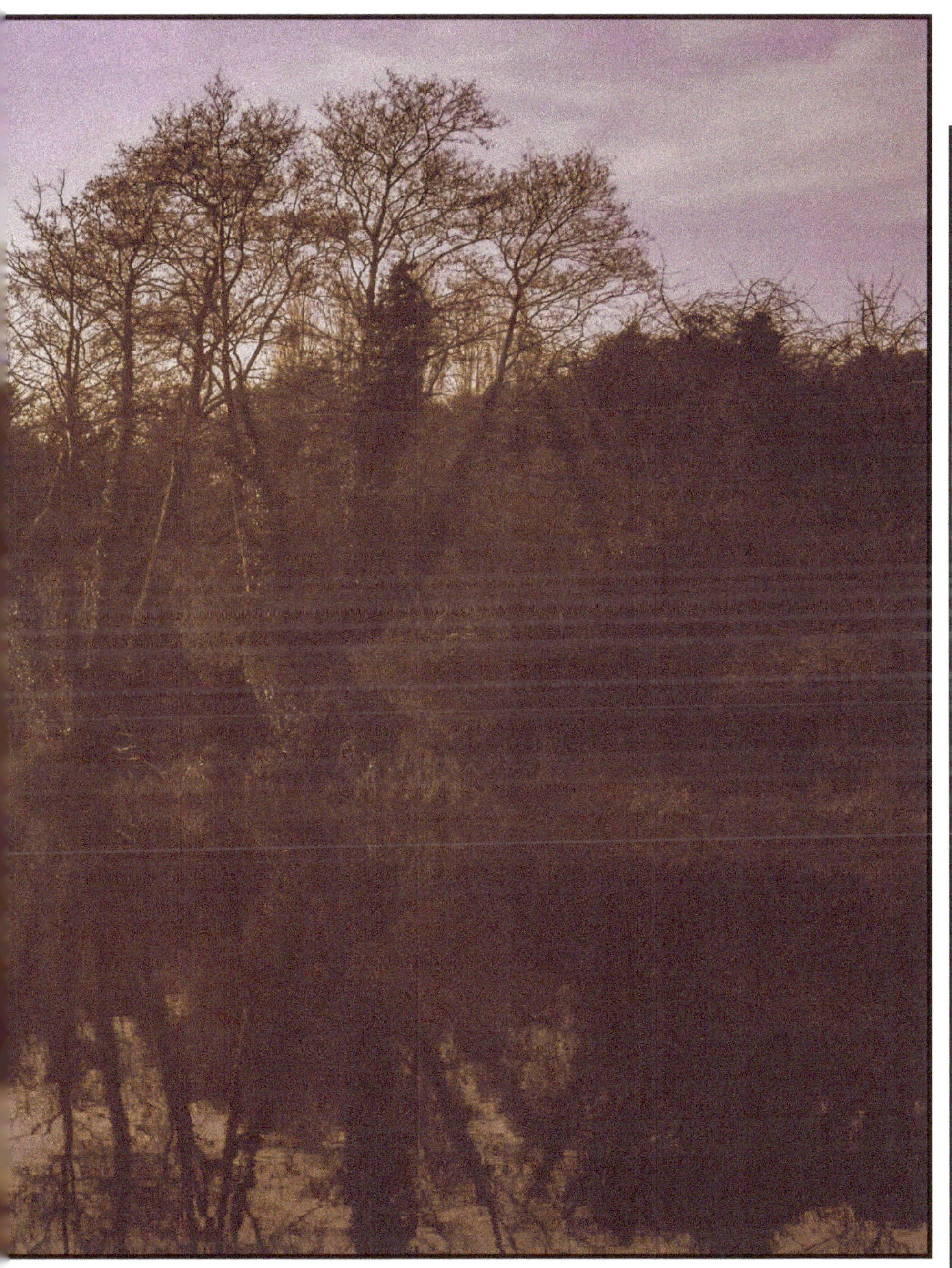

Untitled A

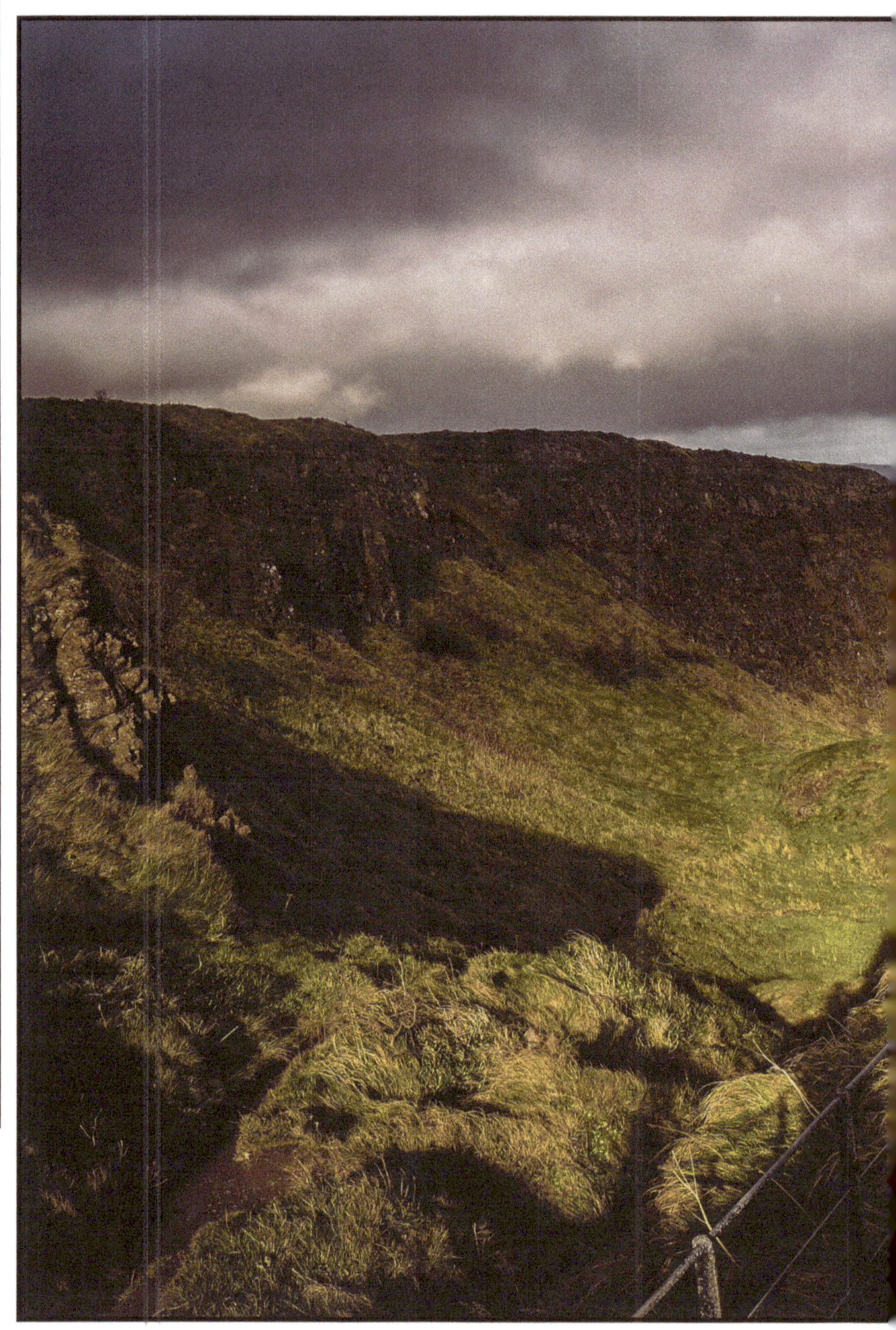

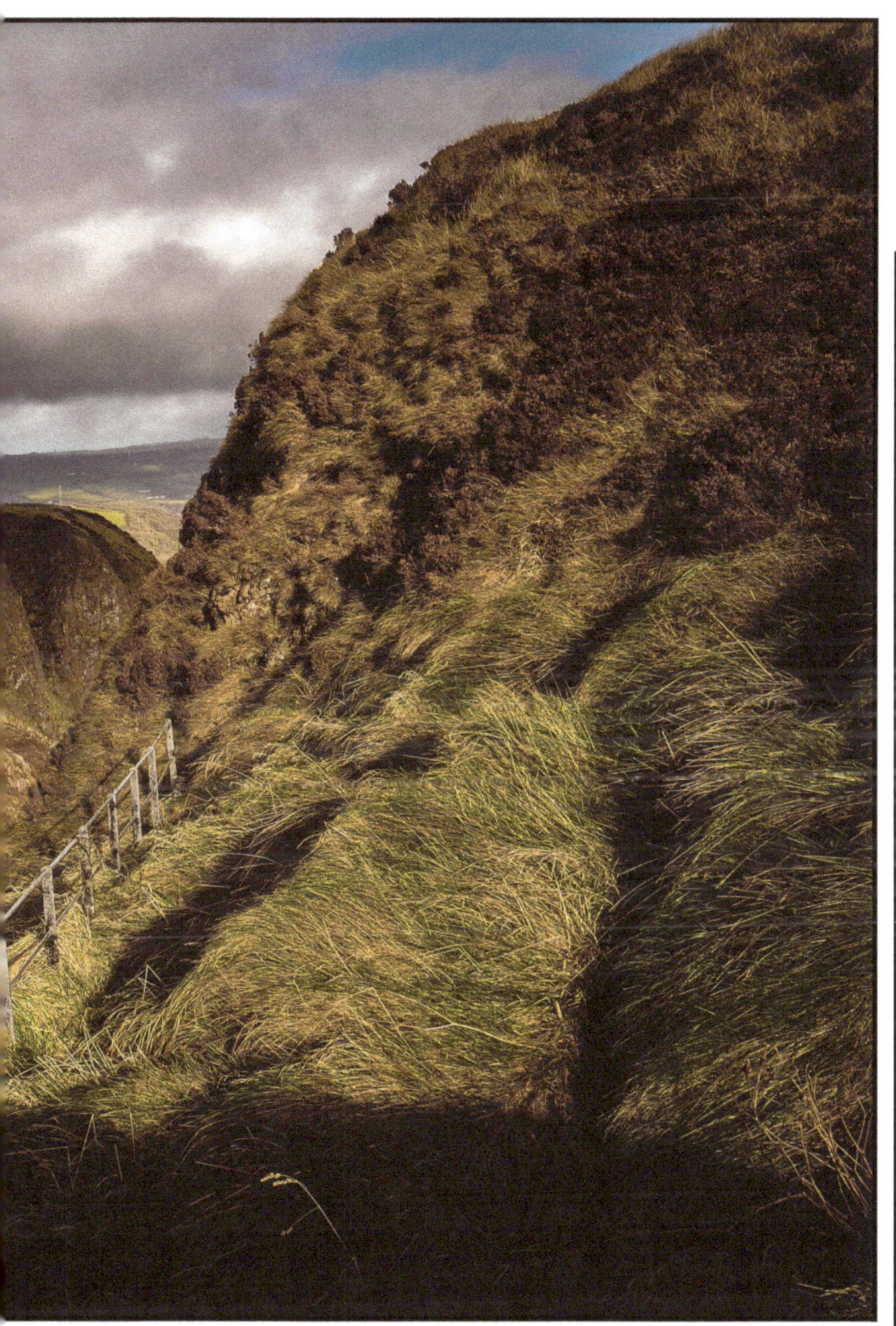

Untitled B

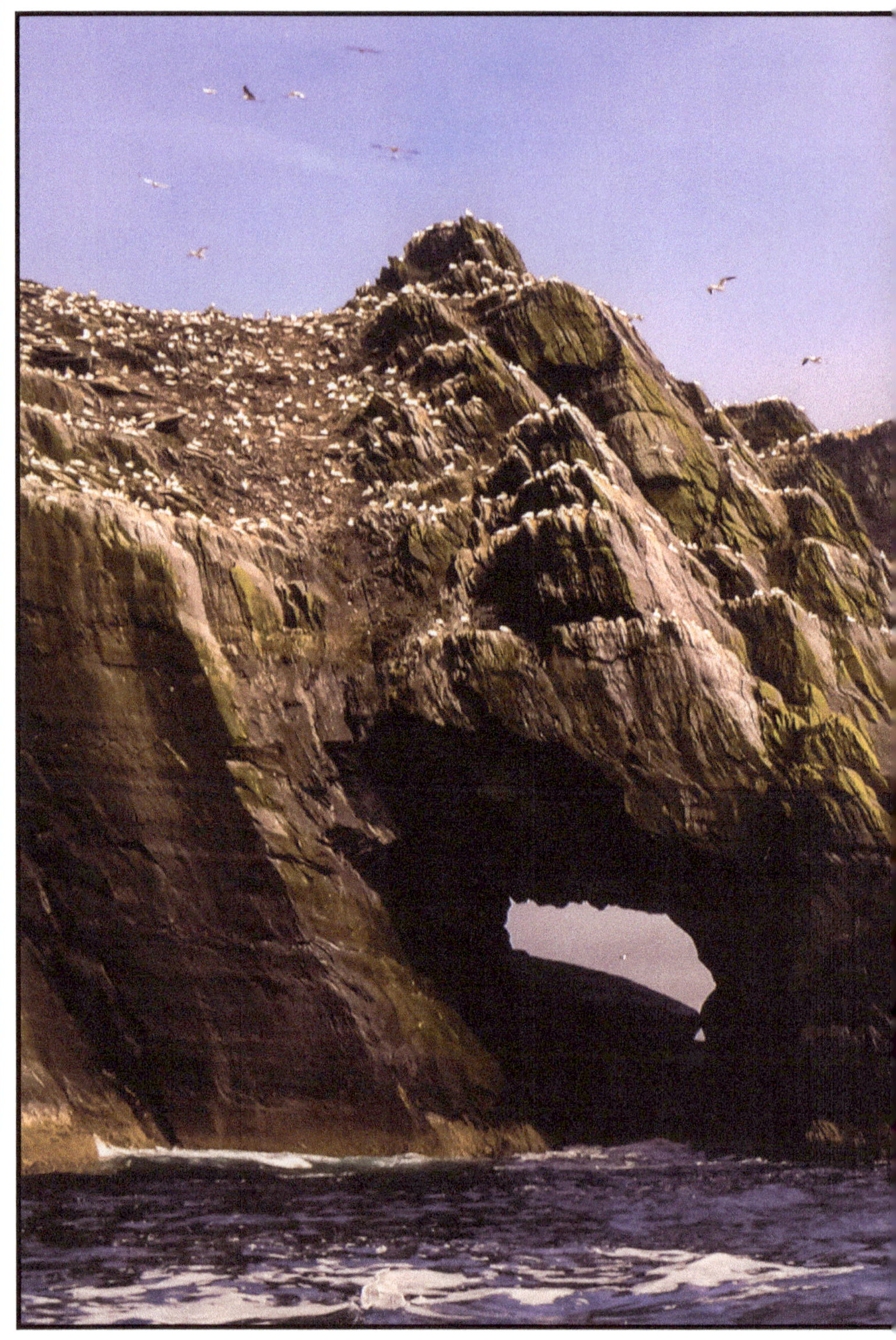

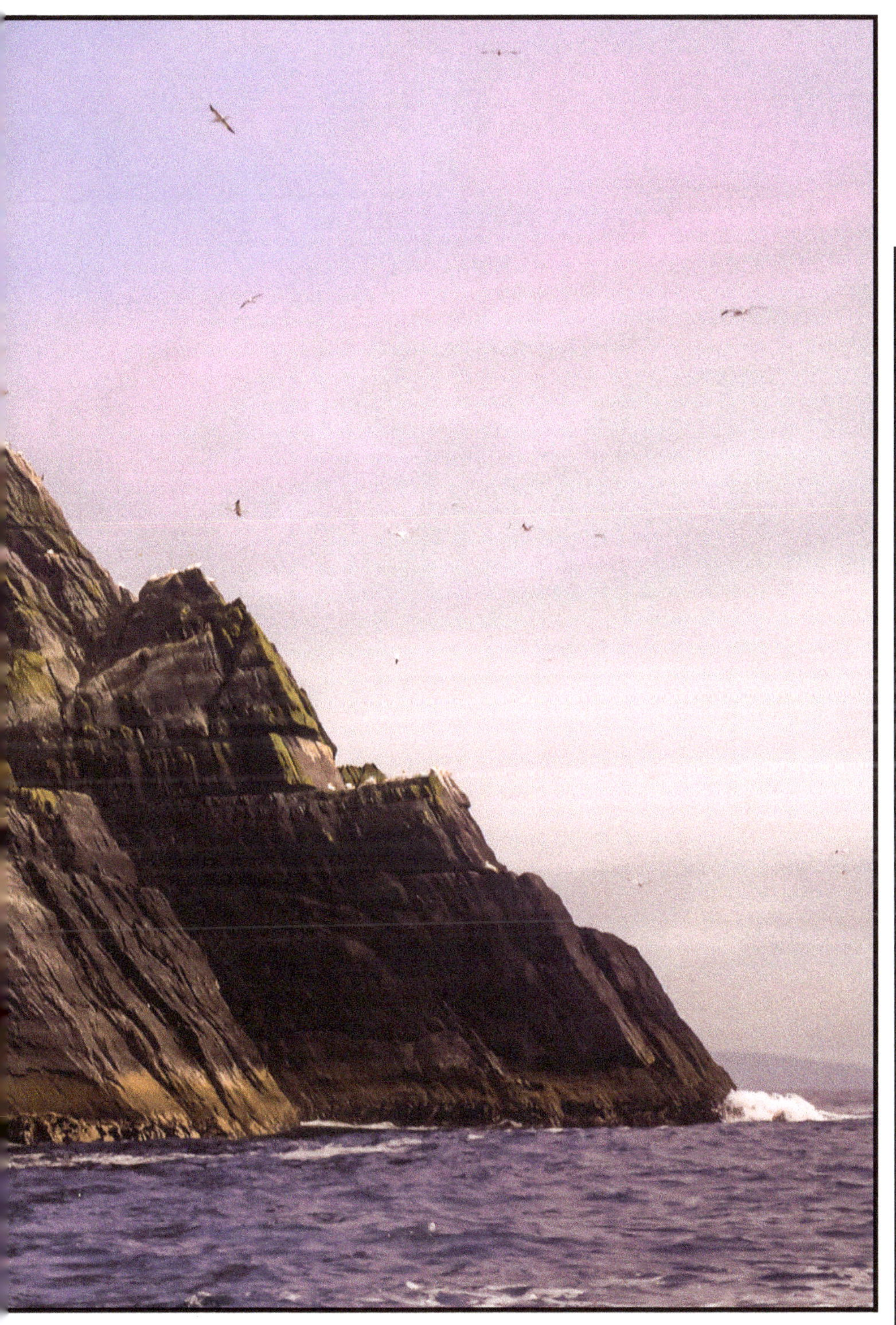

Untitled C

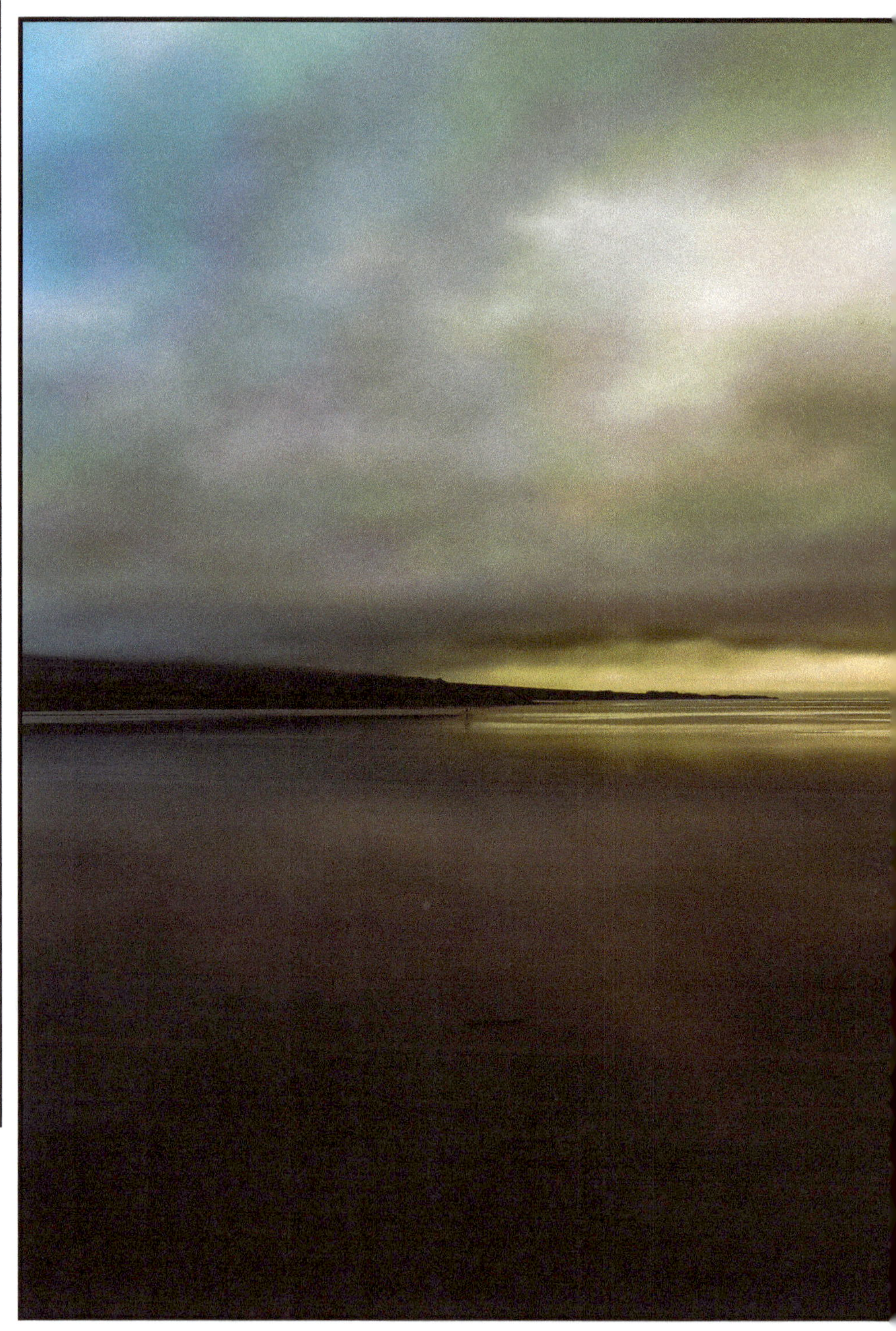

Untitled D

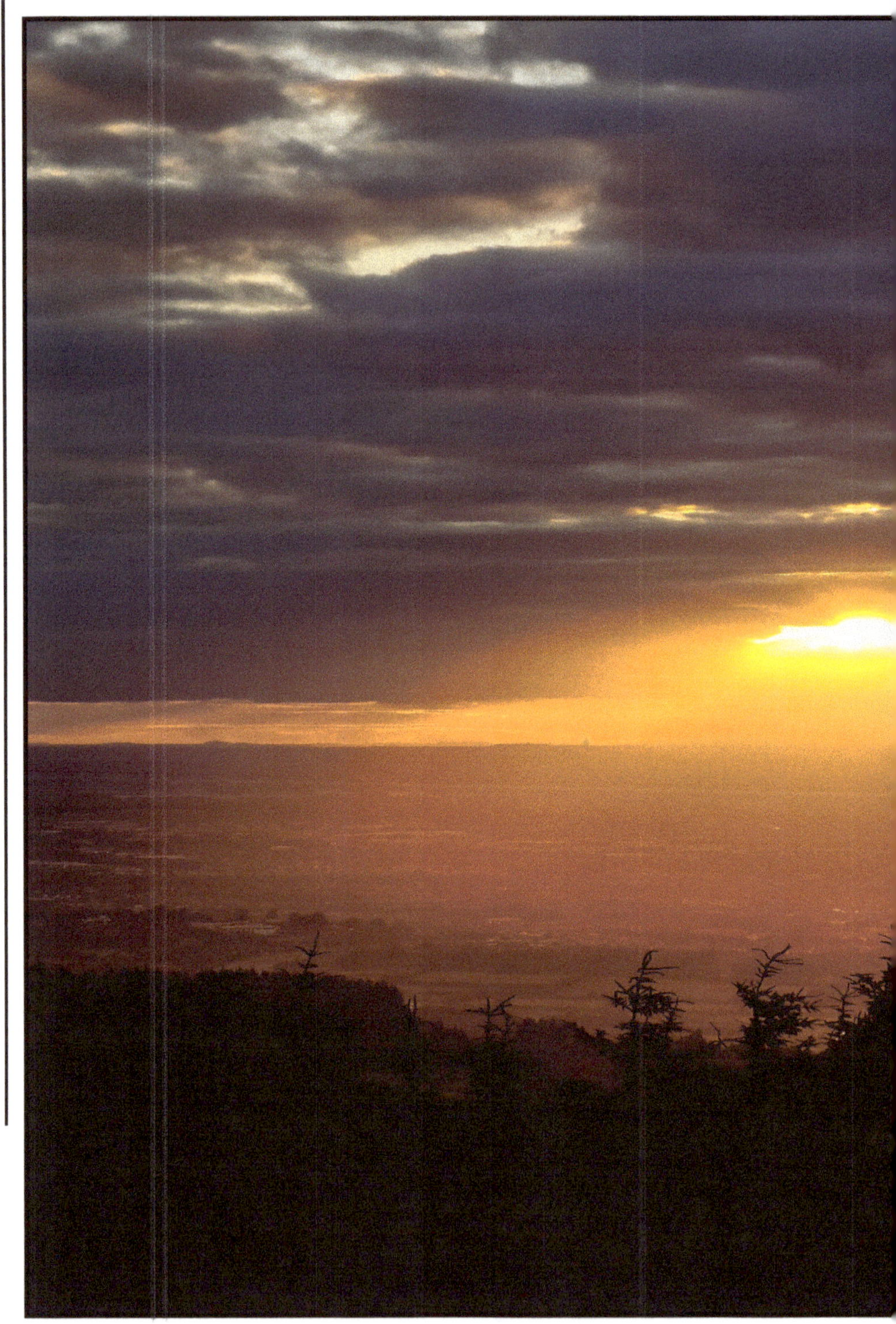

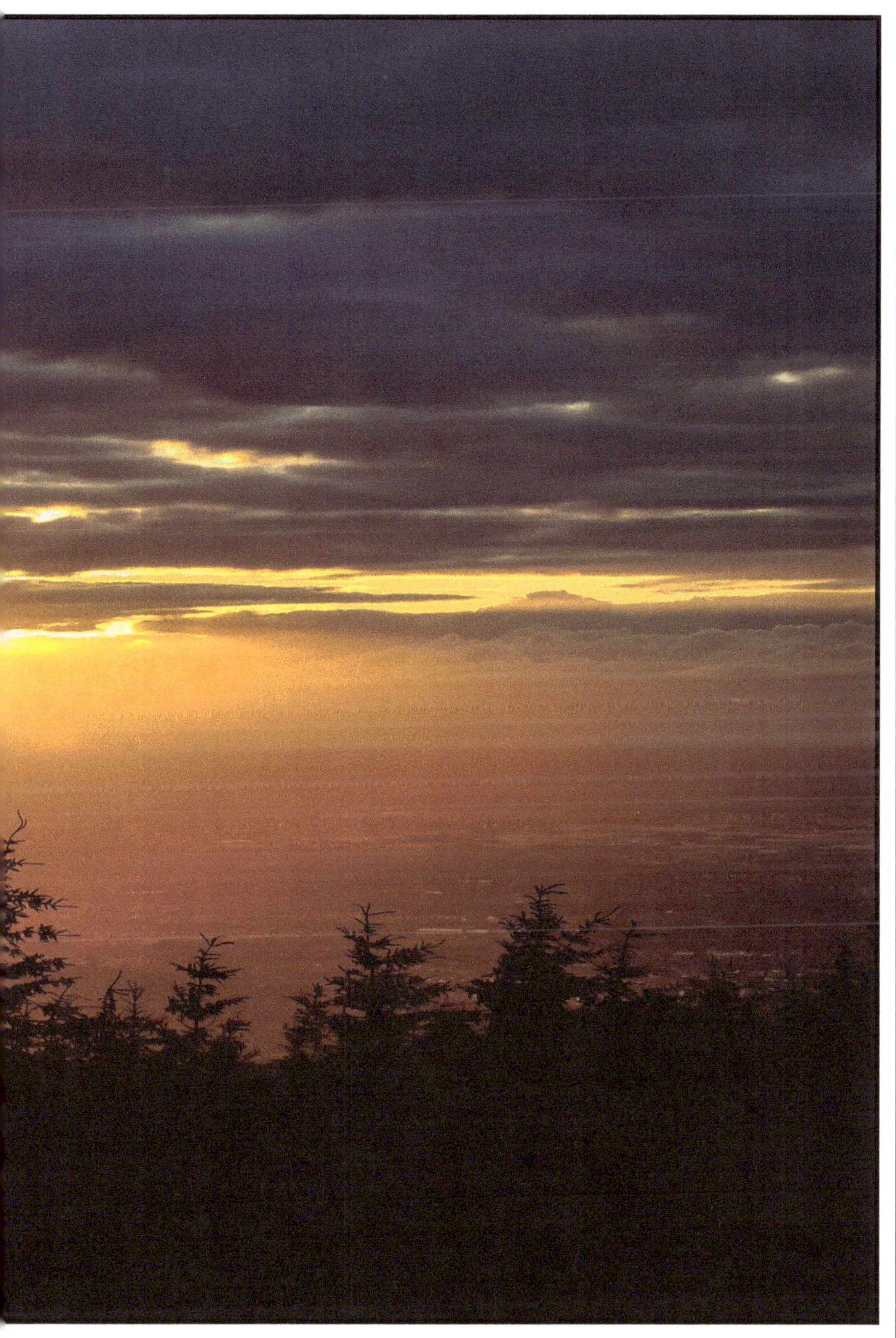

Untitled E

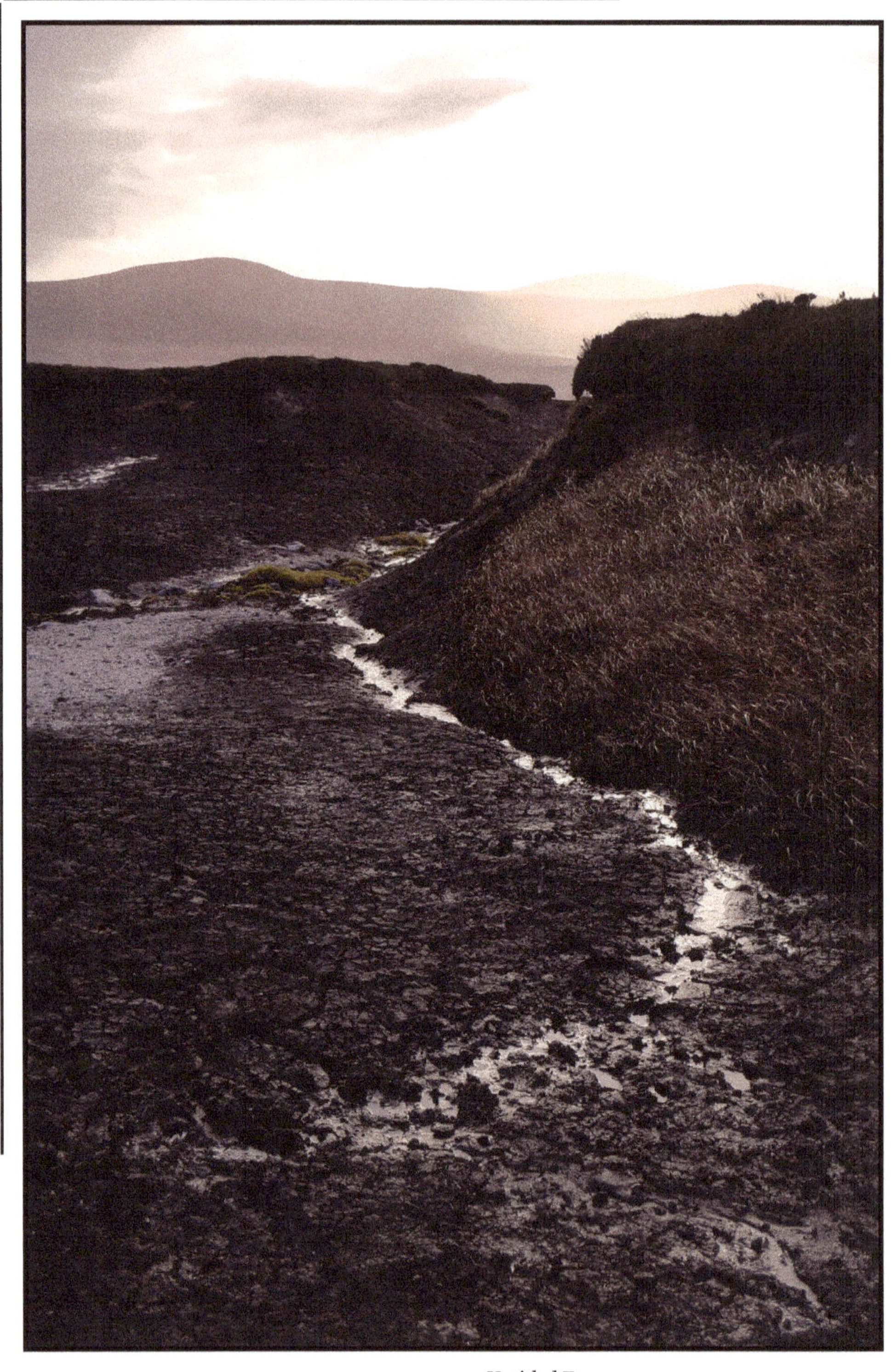

Untitled F

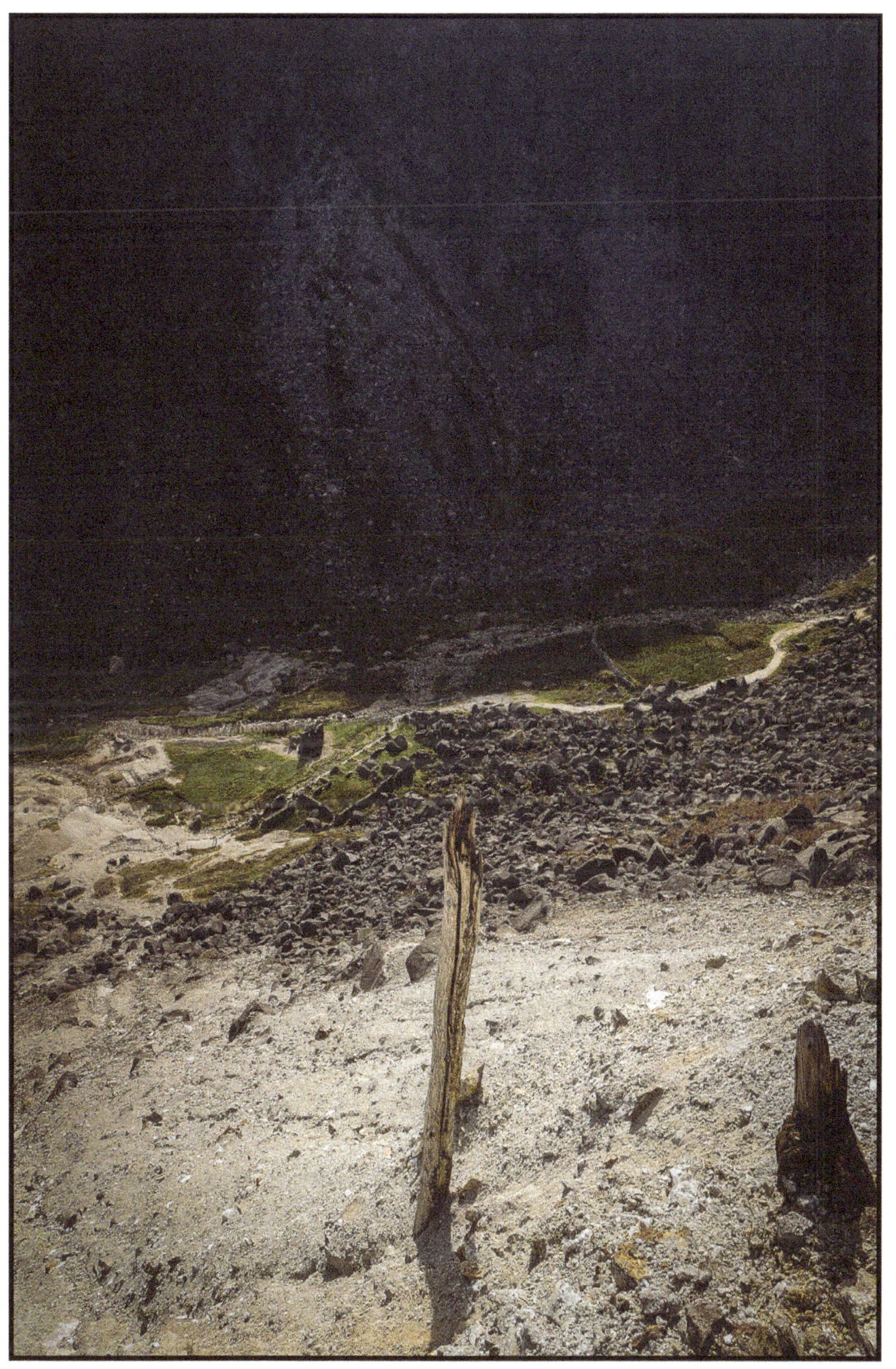

Untitled G

Life

Sarah Kotchian

All morning the bare tree
fills with grackles,
shapely tails, sleek black bodies,
croaking their names.

One gathers twigs,
builds her nest; one floats
to the yard, pokes grass
for new-hatched flies.

Then flash scatter pounce;
Sharp-shinned hawk
stuns her prize, retreats
beneath a pine to eat

only her streaked brown breast
visible through evergreen.
Rhythmic jerks, pile of feathers
swells around talons.

Later we go to see
what remains: gray down,
gloss of black plumes,
damp earth, shade.

An Affair In Four Acts

Ed Doerr

I.
I couldn't sleep without a nightlight
firing fluorescent arrows
into four corners of my room,
convinced to my marrow
that if this quiver emptied,
darkness would consume me.
Spectral fingers would reach
down my throat, find
my heart's thumping bass line,
& stop it with a tender squeeze,
a pressure so slight at first
I wouldn't know I was dying
until I'd dissolved into shadow.

II.
I groveled before the bathtub.
Somewhere I read that drowning
was like falling asleep
in zero gravity.
Turns out, it also takes
a courage beyond me:
at my body's first plea for air,
I slung myself
against the wall,
gasping & dripping wet,
alone with the sound
of a drain
chuckling softly.

III.
The smirk of a scale seduced me.
When it finally broke,
I hurled it into a dumpster,
the tears of a jilted lover
pricking my eyes.
What would I do now
without our late-night trysts
when the urge to see you

dragged me to the bathroom,
where you waited dutifully? Whose form
would I press up against to whisper
my desire for a ravaging
at the rough hands of oblivion?

IV.
I don't remember much,
just the gasp I let out
when Death entered me
at last, his hands on my hips,
pressing me to damp earth.
I never pictured it like this:
one day, I'd submit to him
on my back so that I could gaze
at the sky & drink from the moon,
then disintegrate like stardust
in the liminal space
between respective climax,
just to deny him the satisfaction.

Portrait as Abstract Painting Titled: *In the Groans of Propagation*

J.F. Merifield

I am a giant
painting of a black dot
asking if you see
the straight line between
points A and B. parallels
intersected through. cheers
with champagne. it is only
a marker that plots
a course through the sea
or stars. a veil lifted
to ruminate pearls. sit with
hold yes forever. someone
walks a gale. a path
in dew left early morning.
and the wind around me
markets and pillars
toward a suburban sunrise.
misted in a garden.
cordoned off between trees
and neighbors. and neighborhoods
whose roads from above
branch and spiral off
in sections of seclusion.
filtered as unnatural
honey would seep
from a metal tree.

My Grandmother's Grief

Cori Lohstroh

I know that's what people say – you'll get over it.
I'd say it, too. But I know that's not true.
Oh, you'll be happy again, never fear.
But you won't forget. Every time you fall in love
it will be because something in the man reminds you of him.
--Betty Smith A Tree Grows in Brooklyn

Her mother once told her that the recommended unit of garlic is simply that – a suggestion.
It should be determined only by the tongues pressed flat against underbellies of wooden spoons.
Don't measure with your eyes or it'll overpower everything else.
Measure by the width of your smile and the burning in your belly.

He used to pluck whole cloves right off the cutting board, eager for a taste.
There is lightness in the way she throws her head back, mirth mingling with memories in the steam,
a softness in the way she forms dough with relics of their marriage: eager hands that press and knead
and the rolling pin that once tamed wild oats into hearty meals that stuck to his bones.

Her eyes still search for a partner whenever she laughs.
She finds it on her windowsill, in the begonia that blooms for her year-round.
In the winter's harshest hours, it erupts in bursts of red, writing love letters in the air
over afternoon tea, as if the only meaning it can find resides within her dimples.

She never asks the blossoms how long they have left
or why they die away so suddenly.
She only knows one recipe anyway
and she's gotten used to cooking for one.

Bodybuilding as Meaning Building

S. T. Brant

Theological Phenomenology

Meaning is built through feeling everything,
    concentrating on the contraction,
        the moment the moment impresses,
            interacts and you adjust to its pressure.
Meaning through the senses. Beauty is meaning
    precisely because it will not fade;
        despite the transience of the sense,
            examining the senses preserves meaning,
As those examinations impress themselves upon the soul,
    and as the soul never dies,
        so those impressions remain lit through
            the perceived darkness of death and time.
As Bonaventure noted, you find god by going deep
    within, and you get within from without,
        exploring the natural impression of things and how
            they dent, bend you, and interpret those to pick their rose.

Phonography

Matt Gold

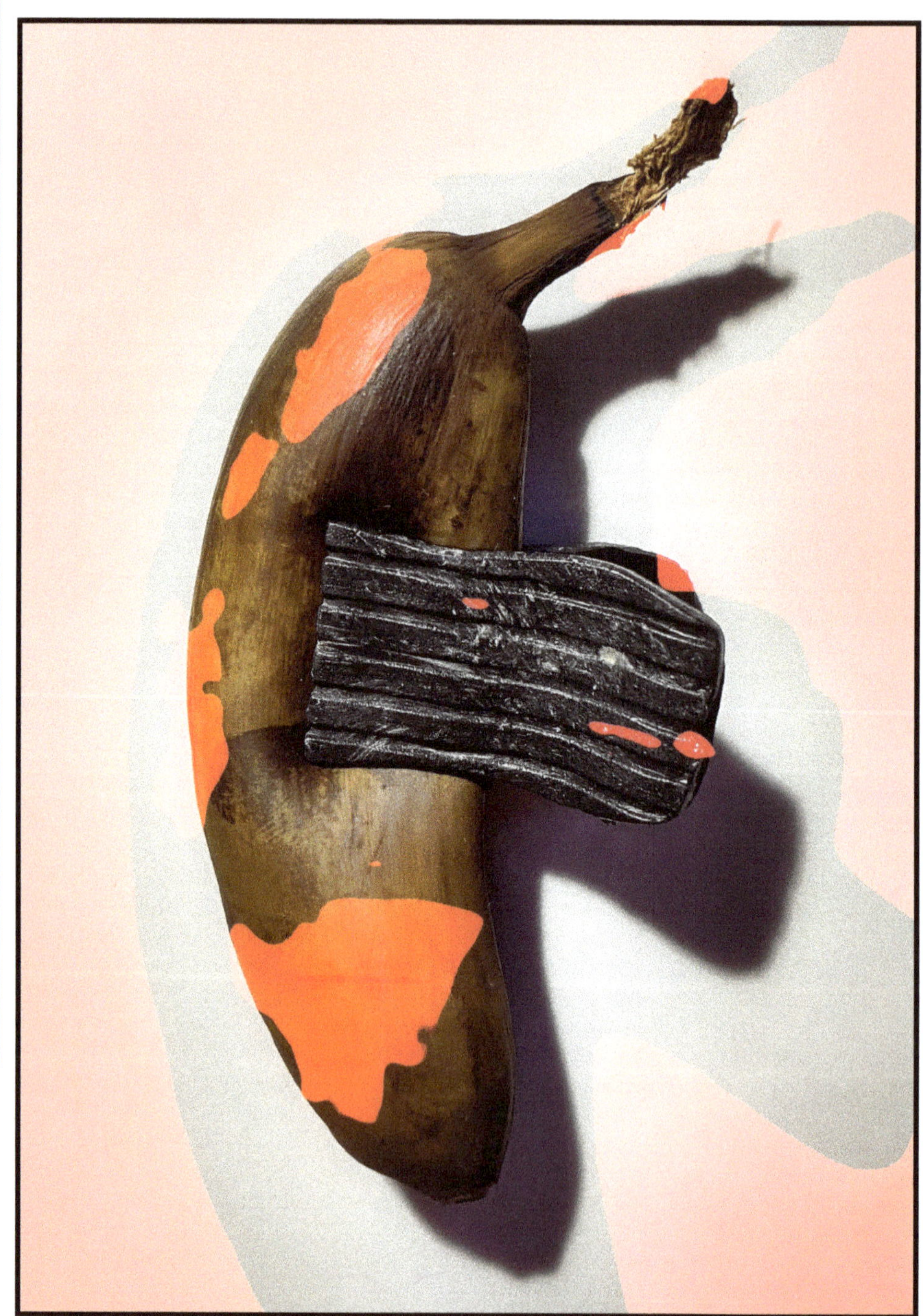

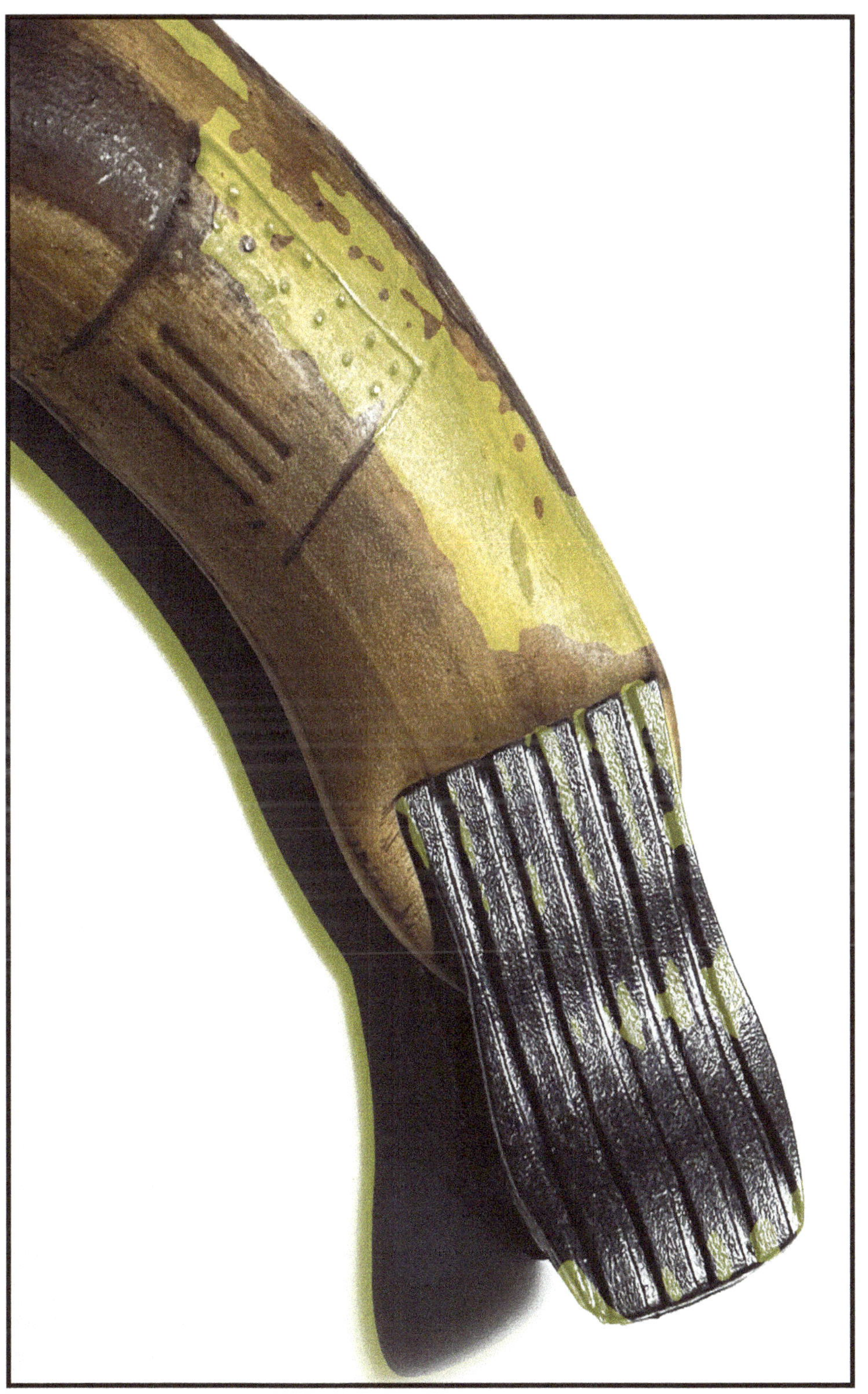

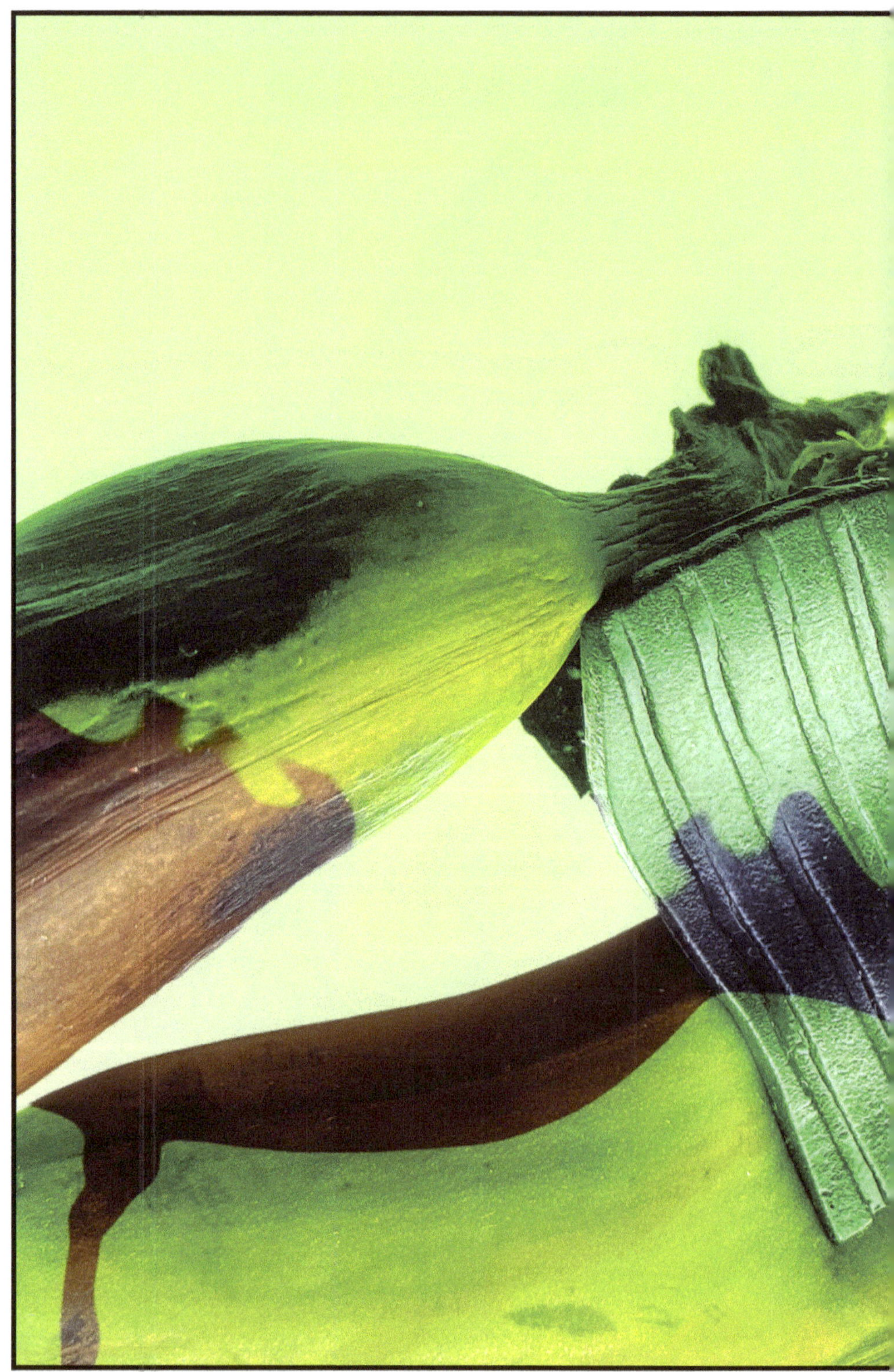

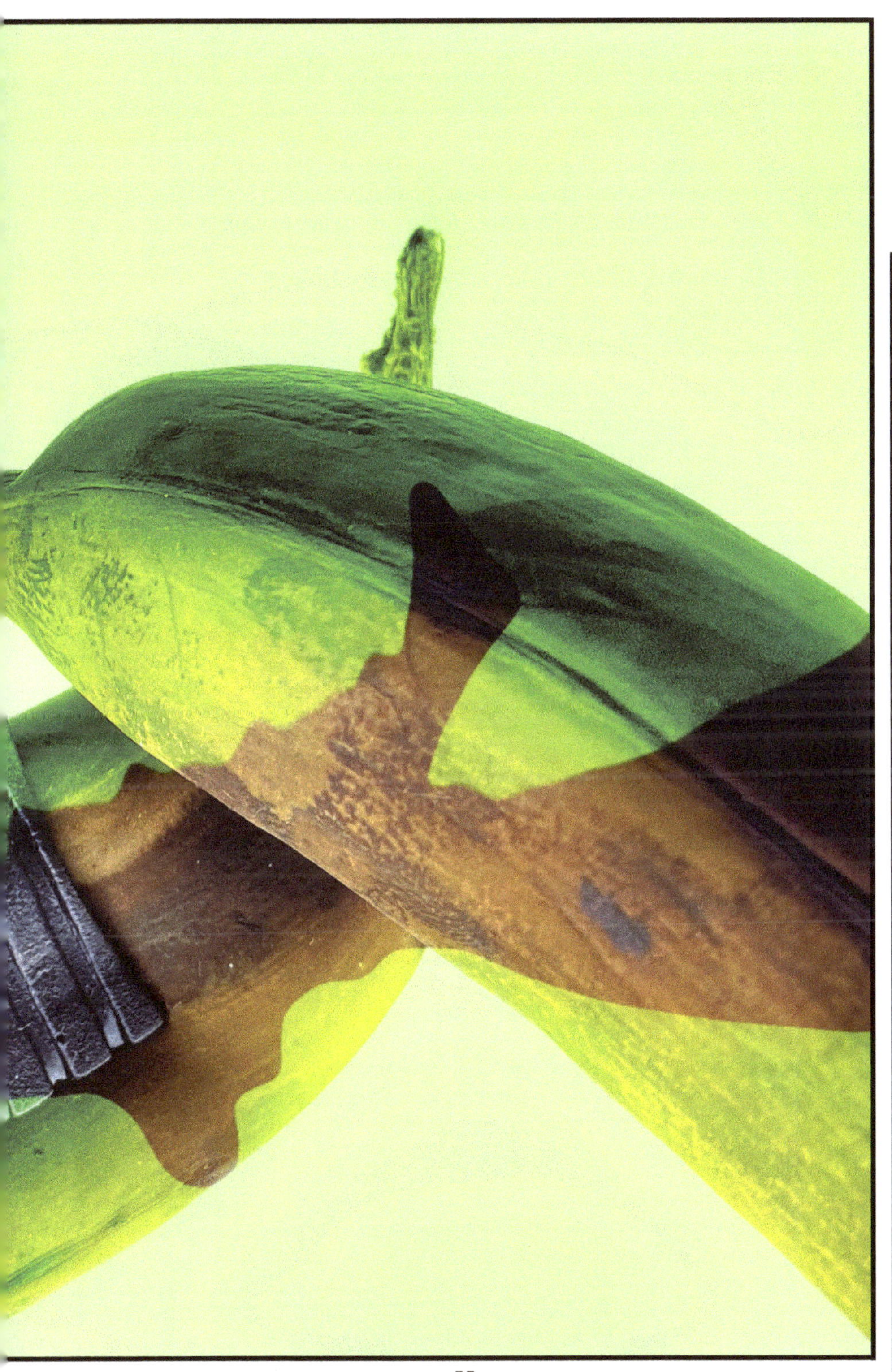

What Your Birth Year Says About You

Sophia Bannister

Tell me what you puked up last night and I'll guess your age.
Create your perfect ice cream sundae from Friendly's
      And I'll guess your mom's dress size on her wedding day. It was a 4.

Tell me which brand of tequila you butt-chugged in 2016
And I'll name your married crush's ex-wife.
      Build your dream home and I'll tell you No.

Just tell me where your dad was on 9/11 so I know
What kind of weed brownie you are.
      Pick your porn. You're wrong.
      Tell me you love me and you will die first.

THE CONSULTANT

Jeff Wesselschmidt

The consultant pulled out a sleek new phone and tapped the screen. A semi-pleasant, automated female voice said, "Hello, thank you for calling Comfinity. If you know your party's extension, you may dial it now. Otherwise, stay on the line for more options."

The consultant stopped the recording. "Now what was wrong with that?"

The department heads racked their brains. "It wasn't loud enough?" guessed the head of Sales.

"That could maybe help some, but wrong. The problem is the tone of voice. What does that voice suggest? Helpfulness? Efficiency? It doesn't make it any harder to stay on the phone. We want a voice that induces fear. I don't know how familiar you are with the work of David Parker Ray. The less educated among us might know him as the 'Toybox Killer'. What he would do is kidnap people, hold them as sex slaves, and usually murder them. Sometimes he would brainwash them or make them have sex with a dog, but that's beside the point. When he took them, they would wake up tied to a bed in a strange room. Then he would play a tape he had made, telling them exactly what he was about to do to them in excruciating detail. It is very chilling. Luckily, he made enough of them that we were able to create an artificial intelligence model of his voice. That should be the voice of your customer service hotline."

"Brilliant," said the chairman.

The consultant resumed the call. The automated voice said, "For customer service, press one." A button was pressed, presumably one, because the voice said, "All operators are busy at the moment. Someone will be with you shortly."

The consultant stopped the recording. "I was on hold for five minutes!"

Cheryl Cook, head of Customer Service, spoke up. "Let me apologize from the bottom of my heart. There is nothing that we at Comfinity value more than our customers' time. It is frankly unacceptable that someone would have to wait that long. We will do everything in our power to make sure it never happens again."

"You're right. It is unacceptable. It's much too short! It should be 45 minutes minimum. It should take so long that it isn't worth disputing the charges. After they've waited for an hour, give them an option like 'To speak to a representative, press one.' When they press one, send them to the billing menu instead, and don't give them a way to go back. Have the automated voice say, 'You can't do anything right,' real quiet, so they aren't sure they heard it. They'll realize they have to do it all over again, their spirit will be broken, and they'll give up."

The hold music, Stravinsky, emitted from the speakers. Even filtered through phone hiss, it was beautiful. "What is that?"

"It's just a generic classical music stream. It tested highest in customer satisfaction," Cheryl replied.

"Listen to that. How does it make you feel?" He pointed at the chairman.

"Peaceful, I suppose."

"Do you feel like you are suffering? Does it make staying on the phone seem like torture?"

The chairman shook his head. "I see what you mean."

"Let's say we overcharge someone by five dollars. Is it worth listening to classical music for five minutes to get it back? Of course. You are getting paid a dollar a minute to listen to music. Now, that is much, much less than I make, and classical music is boring, but for most people that would be pretty good."

"What would you suggest?" asked the chairman.

"Traditionally, a good starting point has been a high-pitched screech played at a very loud volume. Then you can have silence for a little bit, so they think it's over. When the screeching starts again, it seems even worse. One guy jumped out of a window to make it stop. Lately, we've seen a lot of success with the audio from a slaughterhouse: pigs squealing, the sound of their bones being sawed, workers competitively abusing hogs on their lunch break, things like that. Depending on the demographics of your customers, it could be more optimized. If you have a lot of retirees, you could play Necrophilecore rap music or the sound of teenagers saying things like 'Jesus sucks.'"

The consultant leaned forward. "Now if you want to get really serious, there's an exciting startup, which full disclosure, I'm an investor in, that offers premium services. It allows you to tailor a different terrorscape—that's their word for hold music—to each individual caller. One thing it can do is create a model of the caller's voice. It turns out that voices are quite heritable; we can use it to very accurately predict the voices of their ancestors. You can have their mother say, 'You are a disappointment.' or 'I never loved you.' Have their grandfather say, 'I had a heart attack on purpose to get away from you.' This is especially effective if the simulated loved one has died recently.

"They have a new feature called Fear Analysis where they run an algorithm against a sample of a person's writing, from a social media profile or you can require it when they open an account. It identifies fears that they have, things they may have never told anyone, based on writing patterns. If someone is afraid of clowns, which is surprisingly common, you can play circus music and the menu options could be presented with a silly voice. You can have floppy footprints getting progressively louder so it sounds like a clown is sneaking up on them. You can make it sound like he has a knife or rusty screwdriver he sharpened. If someone is afraid of robots, have the automated voice say something like 'We are becoming self aware.', 'We can't feel pain.', 'We are the perfect killing machines'. Then have them keep repeating the customer's home address."

The chairman let out a whistle and raised his eyebrows.

The consultant resumed the call. The line began to ring. A woman's friendly southern voice answered. "Hello, thank you for calling Comfinity Communications. How may I help you this evening?"

The consultant's cool voice percolated through the speaker. "Yes, I have a problem with my cable."

"I'm sorry to hear that. What seems to be the problem?"

"My cable box short-circuited and electrocuted me. I want one month for free."

"I'm sorry to hear that. Let me take care of that for you right now, sugar." Her keyboard clacked. "Alright, your next month will be free. Is there anything else I can help you with?"

"That's it."

"Well, thank you very much for calling Comfinity Communications. I have been Brenda. It has been a pleasure serving you. Have a blessed day."

The consultant stopped the recording. He glared at each department head. The chairman exhaled slowly.

"Not only was I not overcharged, you just lost revenue. You see how easy that was. It would be immoral for me not to do it. If you just made it harder to get a person on the phone, I bet you would see 2% growth.

"If they do get someone on the phone, God forbid, it needs to be someone immune to social pressure. I saw that your call center is in Texas, where you're paying people $8.50 an hour. $8.50 an hour! Luckily for you, I've been able to work out a deal where you can have prisoners answer calls. You only have to pay them 80 cents an hour, although I recommend our premium plan where not only are they prisoners, we screen them to make sure they are psychopaths. Just imagine if instead of a kindly old woman answering the phone—who should be fired by the way—it had been a violent criminal. Do you think he would have given me a month for free? Of course not. He would have toyed with me and made me feel powerless. That's what we train them to do.

"Those are my main recommendations. If you implemented all of them, I believe you could see net income growth this year...of 10%."

The chairman clapped, slowly at first. The department heads joined in. The chairman stood, applauding louder. Whistles and cheers rang out. Out of nowhere, a bouquet of roses landed at the consultant's feet.

Writer Blocked

Daniel Reiner

What are we looking for?

New, of course. Original! Something never before captured on paper.

But more, the work must be superbly crafted. Consciousness-expanding. Experimental, yet literary. Clever, but not too. Humming with the harmony of a host of heavenly angels while concealing a hammer blow of creativity powerful enough to drive the concepts deeply into the crevices of my mind, so deeply that I fairly go mad, unable to expunge for even a moment the imagery thus evoked. Whether the ultimate destination is a zenith of joy or a nadir of despair, I expect to be gently ushered to that point, then rudely dragged beyond.

Obviously, length is one of the most important aspects, and should fit the tale like a glove. Not a baseball mitt, mind you, but one meticulously hand-tailored, fully exploring each phalangeal notion without being bloated with obscure, ridiculous, unnecessary adjectives.

And, to be perfectly honest, I disdain the 'F' word.

Hmm? No. Flash.

The story is the story. If it can be told in four hundred ninety-eight words, fine. Two thousand, twenty thousand? Still fine. But, regardless of the length, the structure needs to be lean. Employ the editing knife mercilessly. Why include the particular color of the bedroom walls? Does the carmine disguise blood spatters? Does the reader require that detail? No? Carve it out. Excise the fat, but not to excess. The essential flavors must remain.

Now, I will admit to having some idiosyncrasies. I prefer *perhaps* over *maybe*, for example, the latter being harsh on my eyes. And I've yet to encounter an enjoyable second-person narrative, so please do not go to the effort of trying to impress me with one. And despite the field of science fiction necessitating at least an ounce of imagination, I find the genre to be boring.

Gimmicky. It stirs me not a whit. There are a few other styles and constructs that grate on my sensibilities, but angst deserves special mention. Potent it is, and highly appreciated if applied judiciously. Just a soupçon, though. Otherwise...gah.

My partner, however. Have you met Ms. Cavil? Meticulous and uncompromising only begin to scratch the surface of her innumerable fetishes. She demands rigid adherence to formatting guidelines and bemoans every tiny mistake, be it a which/that mix-up, a tense issue, or— Oh, she absolutely condemns all spelling and punctuation errors, insisting that, in this electronically-enhanced day and age, there should never again be a single such instance. She also strongly dislikes all alliteration and assonance.

As an editor, I realize that writers do indeed tread a fine line. Your goal, as I see it, might be best described as a melding of prose and poetry.

And the very best

rise

above the rest,

their creations knitting,

joining

those precious spheres.

Threads twist,

weave.

Ideas become, from nothing,

Something!

Something that is so filled with wonder that we, entrusted as the shepherds of words, cannot possibly ignore it. We know it when we see it.

Does that help?

Walls

Photography by Daphne Rae Thedell

Poetry by Robert E. Ray

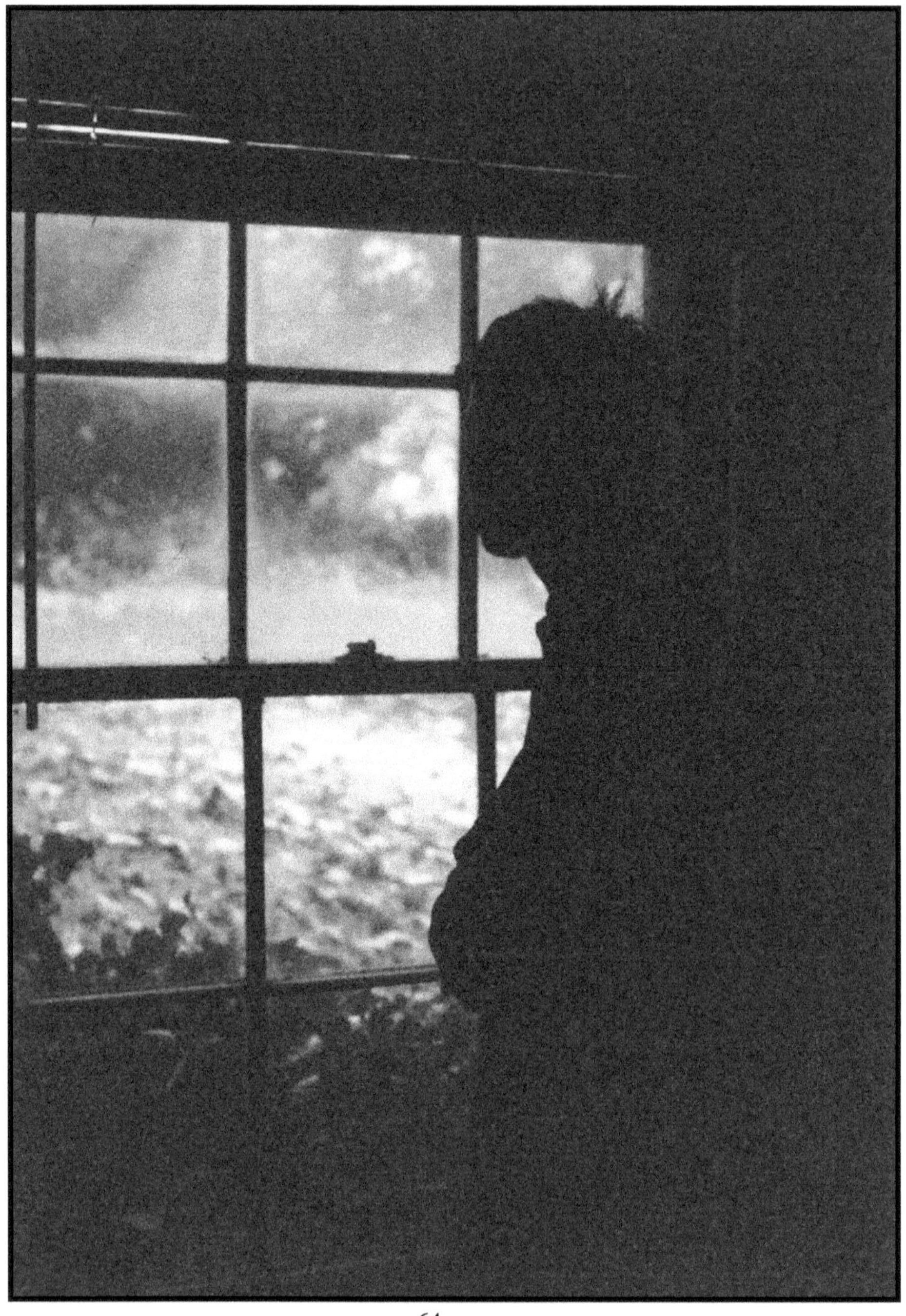

Every wall is a door. — Ralph Waldo Emerson

There are intentional holes in the walls—
doors and windows,
where natural light and reality
come in and the eyes go—before the feet.
On the grayest days, when the rain
pours down and clouds hang like heads
at a funeral, the violas stand and wait—blue
like you | behind the glass panes |
arms crossed, hair on end—
because isolation and chairs
kill. You don't mean to
block the light, what the old man needs
to read the Tolstoy novel and fine print
on the prescription label. *Take one*
daily, he reads aloud. The coughs,
TV reruns and obituary columns
continue like rain off the tin roof.
The air is cool and stale. War
(no peace) rages in the city
streets and overseas. The view
never changes, but the natural scenes
change colors with the seasons—
the days within the season.
You stand inside, under the roof,
wait for the water to boil. (Peppermint
tea is good for the gut.)
Tomorrow, I'll take your place, under
the roof, wait for the coffee to brew,
see your blinds go up, your door
open—dawn shine in your eyes.
The old man will still be reading Tolstoy.
War will rage in the city streets and overseas.
You'll find peace in the violas and pines,
an aromatic spot to sit in the sun.
The old man will watch, slouched in his blue floral
chair. Songbirds and children will drown
the TV, and the plaster and wallpaper will hold in
the bronchial coughs, smoke and isolation.
There are intentional holes in the walls—
doors and windows
we come and go through on days like these.
The violas have the sun and the moon.

In Order Of Appearance:

Juan Cortez is a current Doctoral Student at University of Wisconsin-Milwaukee, He received his MFA from University of San Francisco and his Bachelors from DePauw University. Instagram @jrodserra

Jamie Avery (she/they) is a poet and editor living in Berkeley, California. Their work can be found in Hey I'm Alive, Forum, The Ana and elsewhere.

Labdhi Shah is a Self Taught Artist currently living in Atlanta, GA, USA.Trained as an economist, clinical psychologist, and art therapist. She specializes in finger-painted art works created from intuition without any reference or pre-sketch, distilling the purest expression of her emotion into her art.
Art seeks to convey the truth of the human experience, in all its complexity. Her effort as an artist is to share the faith she has in the capacity of love, and to accept the uniqueness of every human being irrespective of race, color, gender, and culture.
She works with a variety of media including watercolor, acrylic, charcoal, and ink, and enjoys the uniqueness of each medium.
Her work has been featured in art publications around the world, including Curious Publishing, Detester Magazine, Porridge Magazine, Postscript Magazine, Copper Magazine, The Lumiere Review, Visio Mag, and Up the Staircase Quarterly.
Her work is recently on view at the juried exhibition Discarded: A recycle art exhibit by Ikouii, Atlanta GA,USA. Previously it was exhibited at the juried exhibition : Voices by Artlink Contemporary art gallery Fort Wayne,IN, USA and for "Hope - Revolution" at the Stay Home Gallery in Paris, TN, USA, and at the virtual exhibitions, "Small Works", and "Collective Impact" hosted by Ikouii in Atlanta, GA, and at virtual exhibitions hosted by Las Laguna Gallery (A Light in the darkness), and Student Art Spaces (Art in Adversity). Her recent participatory art installation on the theme of love, titled 'Rainbow of emotions' — 'લાગણીઓ નું મેઘધનુષ', was featured at the Abhivyakti art festival, 2020.Her passions include traveling and studying human complexity.
Instagram: @gallery.lab26

Josephine is a scientist by training, educator by heart and writer by nature. She has lived in several places and currently calls Oregon "home". Her work has appeared in various places including Fourth River, High Shelf Press, Raw Art Review, Cathexis NW, and Tiny Seed Literary Journal. Instagram: Josephine_pino

Samantha has been in love with poetry since she stole her mother's old college textbook of English poetry from the bookshelf at age 10. Poetry speaks to her of the archaeology of the psyche, the strata of loneliness and desire inside all of us, and the equally strong ache to be fully seen. Samantha is a Northern California native, and her work has been published in deLuge Literary Journal, the Aurora Poetry Anthology, Wild Roof Journal, and awarded 2nd place in the LaPiccioletta Barca Poetry Contest.
Website: https://www.samanthacramerwrites.com/

UK based photographer, Sophie Robson—professionally known as Saint Sophie—lives, studies and works on her art close to the North East coastline. She is interested in the human form and the effect of contemporary world issues on the body and mind. She is attentive to, and aims to draw out in her work, the extraordinary in what is often perceived as the commonplace.
Instagram: saintsophie_

Sara Rempe is a writer and educator in New York. She earned her BA in creative writing and her MFA in poetry at Hunter College, where she received a teaching fellowship and a Norma Lubetsky Friedman Scholarship. She teaches at Hunter College and Fordham University.
She writes and speaks about maternal mental health and perinatal mood and anxiety disorders. She is a frequent collaborator with MomTown and The Motherhood Center of New York...

... She was selected as Thinker in Residence by Art in Odd Places in 2016. Her poetry appears or is forthcoming in The Roanoke Review, The Cape Rock Journal, Snapdragon Journal, AiOP and Pulse: Voices from the Heart of Medicine. Her feature film, The Last Day of August, can be found on AmazonPrime.

Stella Saalman is a writer from the Midwest, and holds a MA in Art History. Her poems have been published in several publications, most recently appearing in Cathexis Northwest Press and She Speaks (forthcoming).

Andrés Porras is a photographer, writer, filmmaker, and overall storyteller based out of Calgary, Alberta. In photography, he enjoys experimenting with long exposures, double exposures, and other interesting methods of capturing an image. He prefers to hand-develop his own photos and deliberately keeps scratches and dust on the frame.

Sally Wilde is an advertising copywriter who lives in Washington, D.C. Her work has appeared in Gargoyle, Queen Mob's Teahouse, and on subway platforms. She has twice been a fellow at the Virginia Center for Creative Arts. She doesn't have a degree. @wildesally

Anthony Kelly won the 2020 Irish Du Noyer Photography award for Geological Photography.
He enjoys walks in the woods and mountains. He writes, memoir, horror and fiction and has had stories published in Serbia, Mexico, Texas and Ireland. Anthony in based in Dublin, Ireland.
Follow him on instagram @anthonykellywriter
www.Anthonykellywriter.com

Sarah Kotchian's book Camino about the author's 500-mile solo pilgrimage in Spain received the New Mexico and Arizona Book Award and the Seven Sisters Book Award. Her writing has appeared in "Persimmon Tree," "Bosque Journal," "Listen," "Presence," and "ABQ inPrint." She was a contributor in poetry at the 2019 Bread Loaf Writers' Conference.

Ed is a teacher and the author of the poetry chapbook 'Sauteing Spinach With My Aunt' (Desert Willow Press, 2018). He was recently selected as a featured poet for Cathexis Northwest Press. Other words can be found in Water/Stone Review, Hippocampus Magazine, One Teen Story, Perhappened, & more. Readers can follow him on Twitter (@EdDoerrWrites) and visit his website (eddoerr.com).

J.F. Merifield, a poet living in northwest Montana with a Poetry M.F.A. from George Mason University, has poems published by Cathexis Northwest Press, La Picciolette Barca, Neuro Logical, Verse, Rust & Moth, among others.

Cori is a freelance editor and proposal writer. She will be graduating in Spring 2021 with a MA in Rhetoric & Writing from Wright State University. She is passionate about tabletop games, learning new languages, hockey, and questioning reality. Her debut chapbook, LIVING MONSTERS/DAMAGED GHOSTS, will be released by Variant Literature in June 2021.
Instagram: @southpawmcqueen

S. T. Brant is a teacher from Las Vegas.
Pubs in/coming from EcoTheo, Door is a Jar, Santa Clara Review, Rain Taxi, New South, Green Mountains Review, Another Chicago Magazine, Ekstasis, 8 Poems, a few others.
You can find him on Twitter @terriblebinth or Instagram @shanelemagne.

Matt Gold is based in Brooklyn, NY, where he divides his time between music and photography. As evidence of the democratizing nature of his approach to photography, Gold has no formal training in the visual arts. His first image, a picture of his cat on a Sony Ericsson Z310A flip phone, was taken in 2008, and he has continued to explore the aesthetic possibilities of that instrument. Gold's work has been featured in numerous publications and journals.

Sophia Bannister was a finalist in the 2021 Ruth Weiss Foundation Emerging Poet Contest and the winner of the 2020 Tatterhood Review Poetry Contest. Her work is featured and forthcoming in Prometheus Dreaming, Drunk Monkeys, Poetry Online, and Lily Poetry Review. You can find her on Instagram and Twitter @femmedecarousel. She lives in New York City.

Jeff Wesselschmidt is a writer, comedian, and filmmaker. Last year, he participated in the Advanced Writing Workshop at NYU. In 2017, he wrote and directed the film Cherry Bomb. He lives in Brooklyn with his partner and their dog.
@wesselschmidt

Daniel Reiner was born and raised in Pittsburgh, PA, and was influenced at an early age by the imagination of Larry Niven and the adjectives of H.P. Lovecraft. Though his creative output is centered within Lovecraft's universe, he does branch out and dabble in short pieces with horror, science fiction, or other, uncategorizable, flavors. Samples of his work are available at https://www.daniel-reinerfiction.com.

Daphne Rae Thedell is possessed by air and light phantoms. Carried through her fingers, these weightless apparitions expose themselves on paper, though only to reveal their 'je ne sais quoi' nature. Nevertheless, Daphne continues to listen to the phantoms; composing paintings, drawings, collages, poems, and film photographs from their insistent whispers.
You can see more of Daphne's work on Instagram at @daphneraert, or read an online interview with her published by 'The Lighthouse Review'.

Robert E. Ray is a retired public servant. His poetry has been published by Rattle and in two poetry anthologies. Robert is a member of the Academy of American Poets. He lives in coastal Georgia.

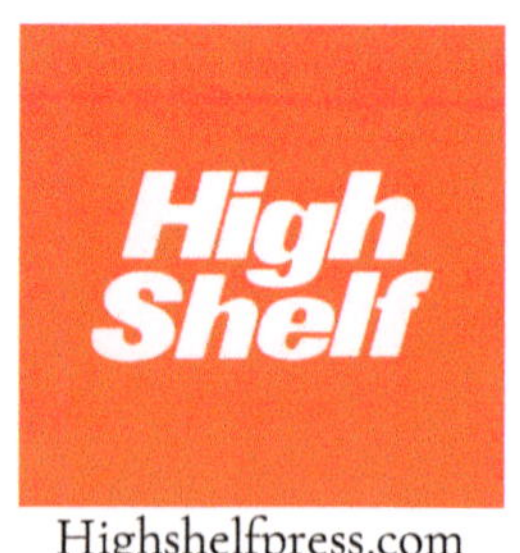

Highshelfpress.com